This record of my period spent as an RAF evader in Occupied France during June, July, August 1944 is dedicated to those known and unknown helpers who risked all to keep me free: also to the memory of my crew friends who died at midnight on the 24th June 1944. A special mention must be made of the following helpers.

Jacqueline Tibbatts
Hélène and Jean Collin
Pierre Galy
George and Mauricette Guilani

Five of the crew died over Pommeréval: sadly the other survivor, Bill McPhail the flight engineer who subsequently escaped from POW camp, died suddenly in 1984.

Bill Knaggs, 1946

The Easy Trip

The loss of
106 Squadron Lancaster LL 975
Pommeréval 24/25th June 1944

Bill Knaggs

Perth & Kinross Libraries

ISBN 0 905452 34 8

Published by
Perth & Kinross Libraries
AK Bell Library
York Place
Perth
PH2 8EP

PERTH &
KINROSS
COUNCIL

Printed by
Cordfall Ltd
0141 572 0878

Contents

Acknowledgements

I wish to thank the following for their support in providing information and photographs:

106 Squadron Association (D. Richards, Secretary and Squadron Historian)

49 Squadron Association (T. Garfield Sec., L. Hay Historian, J. Ward Archivist)

Air Historical Branch(5) RAF, MOD.

RAF Escaping Society (Mrs Elizabeth Lucas Harrison M.B.E., Secretary)

Brian Goulding (*Lancaster at War*)

Msr Michel Tabarant (former member of the French Résistance)

Perth & Kinross Libraries (M. Moir, Head of Libraries & Archives)

106 Squadron was formed in 1917, disbanded 1919 and reformed in 1938 as a bomber squadron flying Hampdens with No. 5 Group Bomber Command. It became a front line squadron in 1941 converting to Lancasters in 1942. One of its Commanding Officers was Wing Commander Guy Gibson who left in March 1943 to form No. 617, the squadron raised specifically to attack the Ruhr dams. He took with him a number of 106 crews.

106 flew 5,834 operational sorties with the loss of 187 aircraft. The squadron was disbanded in 1946. 997 aircrew and 3 ground staff were killed during the war.

The crew of Lancaster LL 975 ZN-H

Pilot	Pilot Officer	Stan Wright	Australian
Navigator	Flight Sergeant	Hughie Smith	Scot
Flight Engineer	Flight Sergeant	Bill McPhail	Scot
Bomb Aimer	Flight Sergeant	Bill Knaggs	Scot
Wireless Operator	Flight Sergeant	Les McGregor	Australian
Mid-Upper Gunner	Flight Sergeant	Nick Clarke	English
Rear Gunner	Flight Sergeant	Bill Beutel	Australian

RAF Station Metheringham – 106 Squadron Lancasters preparing to take-off for Frankfurt on the night of 22nd March 1944 under the watchful eyes of the guiding ground crews. The Lancaster in the extreme background, left hand corner, is just about to roll down the main runway.

Opposite:
Crew quarters RAF Syerston May 1944
Left to right: Nick Clarke, Bill Beutel, Stan Wright, Bill McPhail, Les McGregor.

The Easy Trip

Prepare for operations, 24th June 1944

Royal Air Force Station Metheringham, a typical wartime airfield with its scattering of Nissen huts in the flat Lincolnshire countryside nineteen miles south of Lincoln, the base for 106 Squadron and Lancaster LL 975.

The crew had just returned from a leave delayed for operations prior to and on 'D' Day: on this occasion Les McGregor our wireless operator had accompanied me to Scotland. Saturday the 24th June dawned clear and very warm; mid morning we were warned to stand by for operations. 106 along with most squadrons in Bomber Command had been switched from German targets to attacking communications, ammunition dumps, *V.I and V.II sites in France. Our usual Lancaster had been lost whilst we were on leave and we had been allocated another aircraft from a crew currently on leave, a situation unavoidable but never liked; you became attached to your own aircraft and servicing ground crew. There was a strong bond of friendship in bomber crews; we were all interdependent upon one another and there was great respect for Stan Wright's skill as a pilot. At 22, I was the oldest by 6 months, ages varying from 22 to 18 years, a common age grouping in Bomber Command. Despite our mix, three Scots, three Australians and one Englishman, there was little discussion about our activities prior to volunteering for aircrew. There was a determination to maintain a competent team. Bill McPhail and Les McGregor supplied the humour with the rest adding a more serious balance.

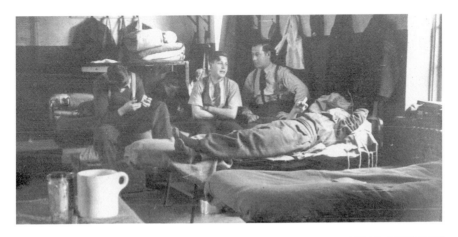

*V.I and V.II , see Appendix

Pilot F/Sgt. Stan Wright March 1944, the first time our Australians had seen snow.

106 Squadron Lancaster at dispersal, RAF Metheringham June 1944.

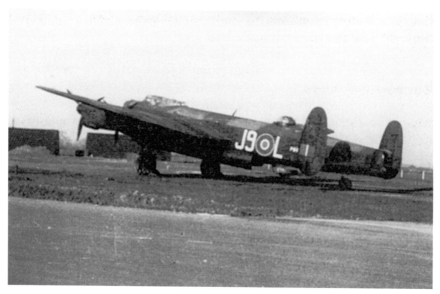

Briefing

Our early evening briefing revealed the target as Pommeréval, a rocket construction site in the Forêt d' Eawy, Seine-Maritime Department, north west France. A 5 Group operation with 111 Lancasters and five *OBOE Mosquitos from 8 Group (Pathfinder Force), the latter to identify and mark target with red TIs (target indicators) and four Mosquitos from 5 Group would additionally support the A/P (aiming point) with green markers. These small targets, often located in woods as was ours that night, required a precision attack. We were to bomb from 6,000 feet at midnight, bombing to be carried out in four waves two minutes between each. We were in the second wave and take-off scheduled for 22.20 hours.

It was a normal briefing with the exception that on this occasion the Intelligence Officer advised little anti-aircraft fire anticipated in the target area and no night fighter opposition expected, adding that it would be a short, easy trip—prophetic words! We rarely heard statements of that nature and were unlikely to have paid attention to them.

Full moon and a clear weather forecast all the way to Pommeréval and back to base, the latter being just as important as the former. Given a relatively short trip on a warm night at 6,000 feet the crew opted to fly in battledress and flying boots. None of us flew armed, revolvers were cumbersome and liable to get caught up in the fuselage when moving around the aircraft. I always flew with a sheath knife and prismatic compass from my scouting days, plus, to the amusement of the crew, two tins of Horlicks tablets. On this trip I left my green silk scarf behind for the first time. It was adorned with horses heads, a suitable motif for someone called 'Knaggs'!, and thus it survived the war.

Bound for France

After the usual 'night flying supper', the precious egg and bacon routine, we prepared to pick up parachutes and other equipment before boarding the crew bus to the Lancaster dispersal points. You had the option of taking your night flying meal either before take-off or upon your return. Bomber crews were not particularly superstitious but with the odds on returning most settled for a meal before flying!

The crew bus dropped us at our dispersal with about half an hour in

---

*OBOE, see Appendix

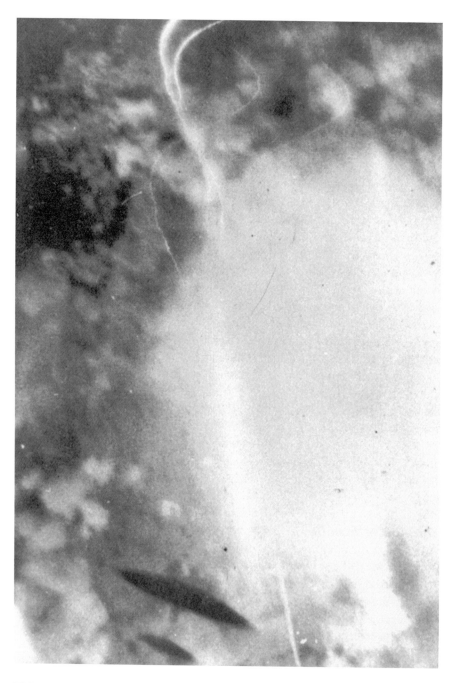

This photoflash released by a 49 Squadron Lancaster over the target at Pommeréval shows a Ju 88 night fighter and is probably the aircraft that destroyed Lancaster LL 975

hand before takeoff. We waited in the warm evening shadows already feeling over dressed even in battledress and parachute harness. At that stage of the war 500 lb bombs were stacked in tiers beside each aircraft dispersal point. These provided a seat, although we could never convince the navigator Hughie Smith that they were quite safe whilst we waited for the Commanding Officer's visit. Group Captain McKechnie always toured the dispersal to wish crews good fortune. This highly respected officer was lost on operations some weeks later. After his greetings we boarded and prepared for takeoff. The usual group of well-wishers were waiting by the signals caravan at the end of the runway to see us off.

In the gathering dusk we gained height over the Wash and set course for France. A night flying test carried out during the afternoon ensured all the equipment was serviceable. A moonlight night ideal for map reading and unfortunately for night fighters, the Lancaster presented a large and with a full bomb load a relatively slow moving target; a good lookout by all was required. I moved my parachute forward so that I could use it as a rest to provide a better angle of view through the bomb sight. Little did I know how invaluable that decision would be.

As we approached the French coast a check with our H2S (radar set) confirmed we were on track; no flak greeted us as we crossed into France. With all on the alert we flew on in perfect conditions apart from the fact we felt very conspicuous in the full moonlight. The target came into view dead on ETA. The red markers laid by Pathfinder Mosquitoes were clearly visible and now backed up by greens.

With the bomb doors open I started to guide the pilot in on the target indicator flares; the light wind assisted in a smooth approach. I could not see any flak, but bombing at 6,000 feet it could well have been bursting among the Lancasters stacked up to 9,000 feet above us. At that moment the sky was suddenly illuminated by a brilliant white light from a flare above and behind us. Lancasters were visible all round and I remember thinking 'some poor devil is going to catch it' on the assumption that it was a flare dropped by a night-fighter. Years later a published photograph revealed that it was a photoflash dropped by a 49 Squadron Lancaster that had malfunctioned and exploded in the bomber stream. The same photograph shows a *Ju 88 night-fighter and the wing of a Lancaster, the latter probably our own.

---

*Ju 88G – Junkers night fighter with 2 x 30 mm and 4 or 6 x 20 mm cannon

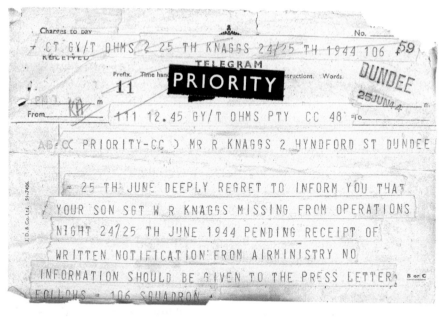

This monument was erected by the local people in Bully cemetery where
Flight Sergeant Bill Beutel and Flight Sergeant Nick Clarke were buried
immediately after the attack at Pommeréval. All the crew members were
eventually laid to rest at St Sever cemetery in Rouen.

Attack

Stan warned the gunners not to look up into the flare. We were now committed to the bombing run; after giving 'bombs gone' there was a shudder and a rasping noise throughout the Lancaster as we were raked from nose to tail by cannon fire from a night-fighter. It was obvious that we were in a desperate state; both port and starboard inner engines had caught fire, warm liquid flowed down my face, not blood as first thought but hydraulic fluid from the shattered front turret above my head. In the attack position the bomb aimer is lying prone so with the turret damaged I was lucky to have escaped injury.

Within seconds Stan gave the orders no bomber crew hoped to hear, his actual words were, 'We've had it boys bale out'. His prompt action saved the lives of myself and Bill McPhail the flight engineer. We unfortunately were to be the only survivors; with no acknowledgement over the intercom from either the mid-upper or rear gunners we will never know if they were killed or injured during the attack. The last known movements of the others as told later by Bill McPhail were that he had handed the pilot his parachute, Hughie Smith the navigator was moving towards the escape hatch and that Les McGregor the wireless operator had been killed outright. Both Bill McPhail and myself felt that the slow quiet way Stan Wright had given his order suggested that he may have been wounded.

Wishing Stan good luck I picked up my parachute only to find that my intercom helmet lines had become entangled with the left hand parachute harness hook. There was no question of trying to release it, Bill McPhail was already down in the nose behind me. It takes time to recount the details, but from the order to bale out to jumping, time can be measured in seconds. The escape hatch seemed to jam for a moment then as it dropped clear I rolled out head first endeavouring unsuccessfully to hold the left side of the parachute against my chest. In the final moments all the time spent in training was justified and meant no delay in departing the Lancaster.

It was too late to wonder whether or not the parachute would open properly attached by only one harness strap, but a severe jolt and crack from the opening chute was a great relief. There was no hope of reconnecting the left hand hook in the air, I was now drifting down suspended by one rigging strap and as a result spilling a little air from the canopy. In these circumstances you have to anticipate a harder landing as you are falling faster than normal. Odd unrelated thoughts flashed through my mind; did I remember to count to ten before pulling the ripcord?, and damn I've left my night flying rations behind (bar of chocolate and an orange). In any other circumstance it would have been a peaceful sensation floating down

Extract from Operations Record Book – June 1944

DETAIL OF WORK CARRIED OUT

By No. 106 Squadron, RAF, Methringham

For the month of . . . June . . . 1944

Date / Aircraft Type & Number	Crew	Duty	Time Up	Time Down	Details of Sortie or Flight
24–25th June 1944 Lancaster JP 663	P/O B.F Durrant	Captain	22.20	01.50	BOMBING – CONSTRUCTIONAL WORKS, POMMERÉVAL Clear, visibility good. Red spot fires and green TIs seen at target. Bombed on three green target indicators from 6500 feet at 00.06 hours. Obtained photograph of the Aiming Point. Bombs seen falling amongst target indicators. Bomb Load: 16x500lb; 2x500lb; (12hrs Delay).
	Sgt F.R Broad	Flt Engineer			
	F/Sgt J.C Pittaray	Navigator			
	F/Sgt A. Buchanan (Can)	Air Bomber			
	Sgt M.W. Jones	W/Operator			
	Sgt W. Martin	M/Upr Gunner			
	F/Sgt R.N Warwick	Rear Gunner			
Lancaster LL975	P/OS.M Wright (Aus)	Captain	22.20	–	Nothing heard from this aircraft after take-off. M I S S I N G.
	F/Sgt W.S McPhail	Flt Engineer			
	F/Sgt H. Smith	Navigator			
	F/Sgt W.R Knaggs	Air Bomber			
	F/Sgt L. McGregor (Aus)	W/Operator			
	F/Sgt A.T. Clarke	M/upr Gunner			
	F/Sgt W. Beutel (Aus)	Rear Gunner			
Lancaster ME 789	F/O L.C.W. Boivin	Captain	22.25	01.45	No cloud, good visibility. Target indicators seen on arrival. Bombed on a single red target indicator from 7000 feet at 00.11 hours. Took aiming point photograph. Bombing was very concentrated. Bomb Load: 16x500lb; 2x500lb; (12hrs Delay).
	Sgt. S. Bell	Flt Engineer			
	Sgt W.S Bryson	Navigator			
	Sgt J.P Nicol	Air Bomber			
	F/Sgt R.H McLean (Aus)	W/Operator			
	Sgt G.E.L Parker	M/Upr Gunner			
	Sgt A. Hargill	Rear Gunner			

Pommeréval operation 24/25th June 1944
– extract from a 49 Squadron report

No. 49 Squadron Lancasters took part in the Pommeréval operation and the following report received courtesy of Leslie Hay, Collator of 49 Squadron Association records provides an eye witness account from Sgt. D. Reid who evaded capture. His Lancaster LM 572, Pilot F/O. Taylor, being shot down on their first operation.

Of the thirteen 49 Squadron aircraft which went to Pommeréval that night, LM 572 failed to return. Three of the crew were killed, three were POWs and one, the navigator, Sgt D. Reid, evaded. In his evasion report he says:

> On the night of 24/25 June 1944 we were briefed to bomb an objective in Pommeréval. We did so at approximately 00.10 hrs on 25 June 44, our height being 8,750 ft. Shortly after 'bombs away' we were hit by flak in our port inner engine which immediately caught fire. The Pilot gave the order to put on our parachutes which we did. Very shortly after that the pilot shouted 'Jump, Jump'.
>
> I left the aircraft from the port hatch following the bomb aimer and engineer who both appeared to leave the aircraft successfully. Before leaving, I saw the Pilot in his position with his parachute on.
>
> On my way down I saw what appeared to be two fighters engaging two Lancaster aircraft. The Lancasters firing tracers from their rear turrets and the fighters from 'forward'. As I appeared to be falling, slowly I spilled air from the parachute to accelerate my descent. On my way down I saw what seemed to me to be three aircraft burning on the ground. I assumed that one of these was my aircraft.

on a calm moonlight night, the reality was that by baling out at 6,000 feet and at the moment of bombing I was now dropping into the target area.

There were a few more explosions below me, then silence. Our Lancaster was now ahead of me still in level flight but well ablaze in both wings. As I watched, a figure dropped from the aircraft which began to lose a little height, then the port wing exploded and the Lancaster spiralled down and crashed just outside the target. Despite all I wished to believe, I realised that Bill McPhail and myself were probably the only survivors.

With a light wind I continued to drift gently down. I could see LL 975 well ablaze lying beyond the target and further to the north there was another distinct fire which could have indicated another launch site or possibly a Lancaster victim of night-fighter or flak. During our bombing run there had been no sign of flak, a sign that fighters were around. As I went through the drill for landing I could see in the moonlight, trees to the right, an open area below and I dropped heavily but safely into a roadside ditch. With little wind there was no difficulty in dragging the chute in and dumping it in the ditch along with harness and Mae West, there was no time to hide them properly.

On foot in occupied France

It was with a feeling of almost disbelief that I found myself standing on enemy soil and apart from the obvious thought 'where to from here' it was a case of departing rapidly from a position surrounded by bomb craters. There were few permanent buildings on rocket launching sites but I could neither see nor hear any signs of life; we had probably taken care of such buildings. The uncanny silence was broken only by the aggressive sound of the night-fighter still orbiting the target or more probably using the blazing wreckage of our Lancaster a few hundred yards to the north as his marker. That night all our aircraft carried as part of their bomb load two delayed action bombs so it was no time to be loitering in the target area. I could just hear the fading engine notes from the last wave of Lancasters homeward bound, for me a very forlorn sound. Now Sunday 25th June I started inland heading east.

I had two priorities, that of placing as much distance as possible away from my parachute and crashed Lancaster, and the location of our flight engineer Bill McPhail who was almost certainly the figure I saw baling out. On reaching the last of the bomb craters I started to call for Bill using the expression 'honey pears' a phrase used in a popular radio programme and no matter how foolish it may have sounded I knew that it would identify me even if it was hardly the ideal location. My route was taking me closer to our blazing aircraft with ammunition adding to the inferno and despite a natural wish to see if there were any survivors common sense dictated otherwise.

Evasion

At this point a motor cycle could be heard approaching at high speed; it would only be Germans so close to a rocket site thus making it impossible to search for Bill McPhail. Reaching the edge of a wood, I heard the noise of more transport. It was now time to distance myself from the parachute and crash site before the Germans started to look for survivors. So much for the intelligence officer's 'easy trip'. After the war I found that *4 Lancasters were lost over Pommeréval, 2 to night-fighters and 2 to flak.

With the Germans now somewhere behind me, I carried on walking east through a fairly narrow fielded area flanked by trees, hoping that my parachute would not be found before daylight. The moon cast deceptive shadows and my progress was slow; the loss of the crew and uncertainty about Bill did not help, but no useful purpose could be served staying close to the target.

Dawn breaks early in June and at first light I was making my way up a gully a few feet wide with fields either side bordered by trees and no sign of habitation. The gully finished in a large expanse of thorn bushes and as it was dangerous to continue in daylight so close to my parachute and target I forced my way into the centre of the bushes to wait and see how the day developed. My sheath knife enabled loosening of the earth to allow a lower profile and such comfort as one could hope for in thorn shrubs.

It was a very clear warm Sunday morning and trouble could be expected once the Germans found my parachute. About 6 a.m. distant voices carried on the still air followed by the sounds of shots; over a year later I discovered that the shots signalled the capture of Bill McPhail. He had landed in the forest and became entangled in the trees; Bill was eventually taken to POW camp *Stalag 7* in Poland. In February 1945 when the Russians were

---

*The 24/25th June 1944 saw the first Bomber Command main force attack on 7 rocket launch sites in the Pas de Calais and Seine Maritime areas. A force of 739 aircraft, of these 22 Lancasters were lost, 130 aircrew killed, 15 became POWs and 9 became evaders. The death rate of 84.4 per cent from 22 Lancaster reflected the difficulties of leaving a stricken aircraft. Intelligence failed to advise aircrews that the Luftwaffe had moved many night-fighter squadrons to the west to defend communications, V.I and V.II sites.

advancing west, the Germans started to withdraw their prisoners back into Germany and during this march Bill escaped and made his way out through Poland and Russia. He was one of the first airmen to return via the port of Odessa. When we finally met at Christmas 1945 it was obvious that he had quite a harrowing time compared to myself.

The crew escape plan assumed that all survived and we would split into three groups making our separate bids for freedom. With little hope of finding Bill in the forest area so close to the target I had no option but to proceed on my own. Apart from a slight stiffness in my right shoulder which had taken the full force of the one parachute harness strap I felt in good shape.

Being shot down over the target gave me my position in France; the handkerchief escape map was but a rough guide. It was a case of remembering the target briefing details and although you listened carefully to such information, you did not view the surrounding countryside with the thought of 'walking home'. I estimated my position about 30 miles inland from Dieppe and some 40–50 miles north of Rouen. That meant I was too close to the 'Atlantic Wall' for comfort and must not move west. The Atlantic Wall was a defensive belt roughly 25 miles in depth that the Germans had constructed from Denmark down the coast to the Spanish border. At least compared with some evaders I had a reasonably accurate starting point.

The voices heard earlier were closing in; the German troops fanned out in the fields on either side and eventually reached the fence edge about three feet above my head. Fortunately they did not come down into the gully to search the bushes and after a few anxious moments the searchers passed on. The ringing of distant church bells added a rather incongruous note to my present plight and location. The increasing heat and thorns made life very uncomfortable but once the Germans had gone I used the sheath knife to deepen my lying position, however it was too dangerous to consider any movement before nightfall.

After my first night in France it was time to take stock. I had avoided the initial search, what lay ahead? We all carried a small escape kit, mine lay in the inside pocket of my battledress tunic. The contents varied during the war; mine contained glucose sweets, concentrated chocolate, water purifying tablets, Benzedrine tablets, button compass, small file, collapsible water bottle and a handkerchief map. We also flew with the currencies of the countries being overflown, in this case francs (old francs). I cannot remember the actual number but the value was roughly £10, a reasonable sum in 1944, and finally a photograph suitable for identity cards.

I was sure that Bill McPhail had survived, but with no idea in which direction he might have headed it was hopeless to search in daylight whilst in the vicinity of the target. My first movements had been dictated by the necessity of covering as much distance as possible from my discarded parachute. The question being whither now and how long could I stay free before finding help? All bomber crews were aware of the odds on surviving, and although never discussed we all flew with that assurance that it could never happen to us. The fact that our Lancaster had been destroyed so quickly with the loss of five close friends overshadowed thoughts of the future.

The Pommeréval operation took place 19 days after 'D' Day. At this stage of the conflict we always checked the latest army positions in Normandy at our Squadron briefings and, based on the details given on the 24th June, I settled for Caen as the nearest battle front. As the crow flies this lay some 100 miles to the south-west, but in practice meant a circuit south to cross the river Seine and probably a journey of 150 miles.

I was tempted to travel east, away from the coastal area on the basis that the Germans would be thinner on the ground, but the thought of a possible early breakout from the Normandy bridgehead made my decision to walk south. I intended to walk at night only, stay on high ground where practical and lie up during daylight hours. Dependant on what lay ahead I estimated it could take six days to reach the Seine. Experience gained night walking on the Pentland Hills with my Edinburgh scout troop had given me a good grounding in navigating by stars and compass. I hoped to find a safe haven north of Rouen to await the Allied advance (not a brilliant idea as the French were to tell me).

It became extremely hot and uncomfortable in the thicket and unexpected trouble arrived in the afternoon when a bull appeared at the fence above my head. I could not see the animal through the bushes but the snorting and pawing at the fence edge was hardly a comforting sound. My main worry was that it could have attracted attentions of German origin, but after a short time it gave up and wandered away. It did occur to me that by walking up the gully and not the field I may have saved myself from an unusual problem. Thirst was the next thing to be resolved but nothing could be done until after dark.

Night journey to Rouen, 25th June

At dusk I headed south on a course that with luck would take me to the River Seine east of Rouen. It was a warm night with full moon and considerable Allied air activity. On reaching the forest edge it was obvious that an accurate course could not be maintained through the trees, making it necessary to follow the wood fringes and make course adjustments east or west when finding open ground. The Forêt d' Eawy offered numerous open areas making it possible to keep a reasonable track.

Progress was slow on this first night; the moon cast strange shadows and I used more caution than necessary by stopping at regular intervals to listen. Ironically almost all the noise came from Allied bombers plus the new experience of being in flying bomb (V.Is) country and seeing a number of these launched. There was no mistaking their distinctive drone and flaring propulsion unit, many malfunctioned, fell and exploded in France. These irregular explosions were to be heard day and night during my walk south.

I managed to stay on high ground throughout the night, and at dawn found a spot shaded by trees overlooking a narrow clearing flanked by trees with a solitary farmhouse some 500 yards away. A rough track lead to the farm from the south and I settled down to watch and wait for dusk.

After my first day lying virtually unable to move inside thorn bushes this was a pleasant change; a situation with good visibility and the opportunity to take to the woods if danger threatened. There was plenty time to dwell on the events at Pommeréval and how short a time elapsed between the fighter attack and destruction of the Lancaster. The theory on the squadron was that five out of a crew of seven had a reasonable chance to bale-out; this may have been good for morale but in truth the figure of two was more accurate. We of course were caught at a bomber's most vulnerable moment, those few minutes when committed to the straight and level bombing run with bomb doors open.

Bill McPhail was a constant thought, wondering if he had managed to stay free, how close he might be or in what direction he had headed. Lying in attractive beech woodland with blue skies and the woods alive with birds it was hard to appreciate that forty-eight hours earlier I was safe in Metheringham and now in enemy territory with the certainty that five of my crew had been killed. The constant movement of Allied aircraft a reminder of the real situation and the not too distant battle fronts.

With the occasional distant sound of motor traffic the only suggestion of human activity, I concentrated my attention on the farm, almost seventeen hours of daylight lay ahead, it would be a tedious wait until dusk.

In the hot weather thirst was a problem. A ration of three Horlicks tablets or chocolate three times a day filled a small gap but the farm seemed my only hope for food. Three people appeared at intervals around the farmhouse but too far away for proper identification. Bomber formations were a reassuring sight except for the fact I viewed them from the wrong side of the Channel. Flying Fortresses and their escorts looked impressive but when homeward bound, left you feeling lonely and stranded.

At dusk after the long hot day I walked down to the farm and when a few yards from the building two elderly men and an old lady emerged. I pointed to my helmet and brevet and in appalling French said 'parachutist Anglais Royal Air Force', with a request for food and water. They seemed rather wary but invited me to join them on a long bench seat against the farm wall. They spoke no English and my French was dreadful, a subject that had received little attention at school. The lady departed and returned with bread, cheese and a large enamel mug of golden liquid, the latter was quickly drunk and the mug refilled. Despite the language problem they indicated the danger of staying locally as there were German patrols. My interpretation was cavalry which sounded unlikely but may have been possible in that forest area. They might have thought I wished to stay the night but I was still too close to the target and crash site to be seeking shelter. It was now quite dark, although with the prospect of a good moonlight night ahead. As I thanked them for their hospitality I realised that the golden liquid just consumed was probably a form of rough Calvados and I felt more at ease than my situation warranted. This was my first experience of help offered without question and at such great risk, for the penalty of such assistance was death.

The family were interested in my collapsible water bottle and this was now filled with the liquid I had just enjoyed. The lady gave me a section of bread with a cone cut from the centre filled with cheese and the crust pressed back like a cork. With these provisions tucked somewhat uncomfortably inside my battle dress tunic I set off on my second night's journey south.

Another night of full moon, warm and little wind, the only alien sound that of the now familiar drone of Allied bombers. The natural contours were gradually carrying me to lower ground and eventually I reached the lightly wooded bank of a river. A slow moving river and about twenty feet wide, I followed it downstream looking for a boat or bridge and found myself approaching in brilliant moonlight a three arched stone bridge. It was difficult to judge the width of road carried but watching and listening I was uneasy about the silence and possible guards. Skimming two flat stones across the water produced no reaction. Still uncertain I backtracked out of sight and stepped into the river. It was waist deep and I waded until out of my depth then swam the short middle section. I was not a very good swimmer but my main fear was the risk of losing my flying boots. Swimming fully dressed was hardly ideal but there was little option, and the far bank was safely reached. The bread and cheese so kindly given had become a soggy mess, it was a very wet airman that kept moving until daylight. Unknown to me then the river I had just crossed was the Varenne.

Finding a site on hilly ground with cover from surrounding bushes I

The Easy Trip

Walking directly south from Pommeréval carried me to a hamlet on the Seine east of Rouen. The Résistance then drove me north through Rouen to Houppeville, the pick up point for transport to Paris.

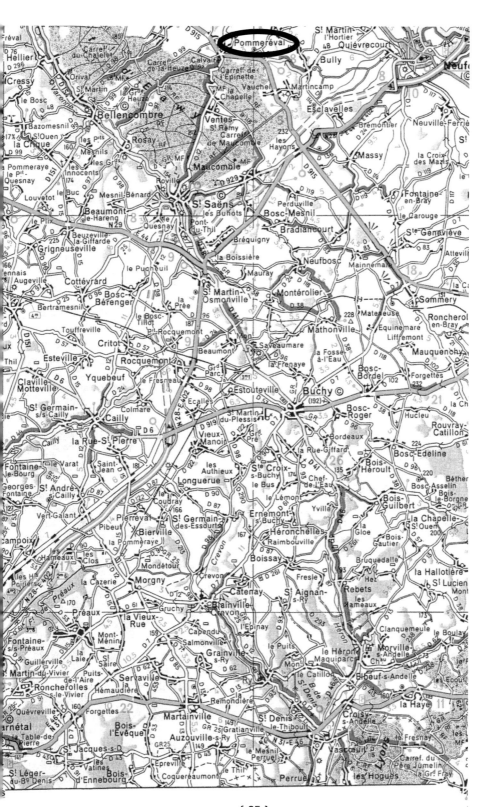

was able to strip off as soon as the sun became warm enough and spent the heat of the day in my underpants with the rest of my clothing scattered around which with the exception of the flying boots linings dried out completely. I must have looked an odd sight from the air and was indeed fortunate that it was summer time. For the first time I could see in the distance what might have been a large village or small town. As it lay to the east and therefore closer to the Atlantic Wall defence line it would probably be a base for German troops and of no help to me. My state of undress meant being more alert than usual, should a rapid departure be necessary. It would be a long tedious wait for dusk, broken only by the steady activities of our bombers and V.Is.

In the late afternoon storm clouds appeared in the south, a bad omen for the night ahead. At dusk the storm broke with heavy thunder, torrential rain and spectacular lightning. By midnight, drenched and following the edge of a wood, I heard movement in front, stopped, waited and with the next flash of lightning found myself looking at a large wild boar about six feet away. Fortunately with the following clap of thunder it turned back into the trees. In the split seconds you have with lightning it was enough to identify the boar with business-like tusks. In later years I found that the Forêt d' Eawy, one of three renowned beech woodlands lying between the valleys of the Varenne and the river Béthune, was until 1939 the last great boar hunting forest in France. Many hazards had been anticipated, mainly of German origin, but certainly not wildlife.

The storm continued all night and, completely soaked, I started moving to lower ground in search of shelter. Out of the dark a farmhouse appeared and it seemed to be an isolated building. Walking round the farm I noticed a small shed. With little point pressing on in such a wet state I entered the shed and from what could be felt in the darkness it was partially filled with logs. Closing the door I removed my battledress tunic and fell asleep against the logs.

Some time after dawn I was awakened by the door opening and a middle aged lady entered carrying a basket. She was obviously startled to find that overnight she had gained an unexpected and probably unwelcome visitor. She did not speak English but I explained that I was an RAF parachutist. She made it clear that I must not leave the shed or open the door and that she would return. It is surprising what you can do with sign language!

I think for a moment I did her the injustice of wondering whether I was in safe hands before she returned shortly with the basket now covered with a cloth and inside a large white bowl of boiling milk full of small squares of bread. In my damp state, my first hot meal in France was more than appreciated and it certainly lifted my spirits. The lady departed with some logs saying her husband would join me later.

When her husband appeared I gave him such information as necessary to prove my identity. This was essential as they risked certain death by helping me, even for providing food. The Germans were using their own people dressed in RAF uniform to trap such helpers and also to try to infiltrate the escape routes to the south. In situations like this you did not ask the names of helpers or your exact position; what you did not know you could not divulge. With a further reminder not to move outside, the farmer opened the door slightly so that I could see through the gap between the door frame and the hinged side. There a few hundred yards away across open ground which I had not seen in the dark and the rain lay a small cottage. He shrugged his shoulders and said, 'Collaborators'. It was a timely reminder of the fine line between luck and disaster. In all Occupied countries there were those not prepared to take risks and those who would betray for a reward, it was ever thus: (reward 10,000 francs).

In the afternoon the farmer and his wife returned with a bowl of soup and bread. They produced a school atlas, and having indicated my possible position they nodded although the scale was of little help. They were alarmed to find that I was heading for Rouen stating that it was too dangerous.

They wanted me to leave my uniform and to provide me with civilian clothes. However, a few days into France I was reluctant to part company with my uniform on the basis that at this stage, if I ran the risk of being shot, it might as well be as a member of the RAF. I was given an old pair of trousers, jacket, raincoat and a haversack and put the clothes on over my uniform.

It was a hot day in the cramped log shed but the heat did help to dry my clothes. The long hours gave time for mixed thoughts; it concerned me that my parents would only know that I was posted missing; the continual question about the whereabouts of Bill McPhail the flight engineer; above all the certainty that the rest of the crew had been killed. We, like so many bomber crews, represented a band of very close friends.

That evening when it was dark enough not to be seen from the cottage, the farmer and his wife arrived with the small haversack filled with bread, cheese and the water bottle filled with what seemed to be cider. My sincere thanks were only limited by my poor French. The lady asked if she could have my flying helmet; it was the only thing I had to give for we carried no personal effects on operations and it was handed over with great pleasure. Walking away with their good wishes I was troubled by the fact that if the farm was ever searched and the helmet found they would have been shot. Their courageous example was to be repeated many times before my

AVIS

Toute personne du sexe masculin qui aiderait, directement ou indirectement, les équipages d'avions ennemis descendus en parachute, ou ayant fait un atterrissage forcé, favoriserait leur fuite, les cacherait ou leur viendrait en aide de quelque façon que ce soit, sera fusillée sur le champ.

Les femmes qui se rendraient coupables du même délit seront envoyées dans des camps de concentration situés en Allemagne.

Les personnes qui s'empareront d'équipages contraints a atterrir, ou de parachutistes, ou qui auront contribué, par leur attitude, à leur capture, recevront une prime pouvant aller jusqu'à **10.000** francs. Dans certains cas particuliers, cette récompense sera encore augmentée.

Paris, le 22 Septembre 1941.

Le Militärbefehlshaber en France.
Signé : von **STÜLPNAGEL**
Général d'Infanterie.

TRANSLATION: *Any male person directly or indirectly helping the crew of enemy aircraft landed by parachute or having effected a forced landing, or assisting in their evasion, or hiding and helping them in any way whatever, will be shot immediately.*

Women guilty of the same offence will be deported to concentration camps in Germany.

Any persons seizing crew members having effected a forced landing or descended by parachute, or who, by their attitude, contribute to their capture, will receive a reward of up to 10,000 francs. In some special cases this reward will be even higher.

Paris, 22nd September 1941.
The Military Governor in France
Signed: von Stülpnagel, Infantry General

journey's end and unfortunately they were one of the families I was unable to trace after the war.

With the forest behind me and moving in more open countryside my route was suddenly blocked by an extensive area of corn (my assumption in the limited light). Carrying on through the corn, a flicker of light brought me to a halt. Dropping out of sight and listening I could hear faint voices, and becoming used to the changing shadows picked out the outline of vehicles ahead stationary on a road. That faint light may have been a soldier with a cigarette and probably saved me from capture. It must have been a German column at rest; judging distance in that light was difficult but I was much too close for safety. Turning to retrace my steps I was shocked to find that I had left a broad swathe in the corn that stood out clearly in the moonlight. It was a lesson for the future and a mistake that a boy scout should not have made!

Moving on south in the undulating landscape with dark patches that indicated small woods it seemed uncanny that I had so little sight of German forces or for that matter towns or villages. Movement at night restricted my outlook and by day I was limited by the protective screen around my hiding place. A constant reminder of time and place were the Flying Bombs (V.Is) and Allied aircraft.

Shortly after my cornfield experience I heard the familiar sound of Lancaster engines and at what may have been a mile or two ahead TIs (target indicators) were dropped. These were followed by a short but heavy bombing attack; it must have been another V.II rocket site. Watching at this close range it was an impressive if unusual situation being on the wrong end of an RAF raid. Unfortunately it also meant a detour to avoid the target area. After an eventful night I looked forward to finding a sheltered spot at daybreak.

29th June, another vantage point at dawn with good cover. Despite a reasonable view, no obvious sign of any town or village although from time to time the sound of distant traffic and always the accompaniment of Allied bombers and the despatch of V.Is heading west. Our fighter-bombers were now seen in greater numbers going south. With my fourth night behind me our fighter activity surely meant that I was close to the Seine.

Food consisted of three Horlicks tablets thrice daily. I doubt that it did much for my appetite but it helped to space out the daylight hours. During the night I had crossed two small streams, managing to fall in each but at least filled the water bottle, the state of the water rather dubious but the purifying tablets gave some assurance. The old raincoat proved a great boon deflecting as it did the dawn chill and moisture before the sun began to warm things up.

With increasing tiredness I felt that less progress was being made at night. My flying boot linings never fully dried out and the woollen insoles had achieved a corrugated effect which made for uncomfortable walking. The boots were of a pattern that meant I could cut the tops loose and be left with a pair of shoes, I kept them intact however to support my ankles.

It seemed an age since I had dropped into France and with no knowledge of the state of the invasion, early contact with the French was required; the food situation made this essential. I had considered various options as I walked south including moving east away from the battle front but now hoped to find shelter near the Seine to await the Allied breakout from the Normandy bridgehead. Another long hot day enabled me to dry out damp trousers and at dusk moved out on what I hoped might be my last night walking.

The moon no longer full but still providing adequate light, I continued my pattern of stopping at intervals to listen. Now clear of the Forêt d' Eawy it was easier to maintain a more accurate course but it would still be guesswork as to whether I could strike the Seine east or west of Rouen.

Making my way down a gentle slope, I spotted in the moonlight ahead an aircraft that had made a very good belly landing in the sense it seemed almost intact. Getting closer and lying down in case of guards, it was now clear it was a *Me 109. The canopy was closed but in what must have been a trick of the light there was an impression of a pilot's head. The state of the Me 109 suggested a recent crash. I waited for a short time to ensure no guards in the vicinity then moved away as quietly as possible to level ground.

Just after midnight I arrived at a hamlet of small cottages set either side of a country road with no sign of activity. The cottages nearest to me had fairly long if narrow back gardens. I decided to check the closest gardens in the hope of finding something edible. It was almost impossible to identify anything in the moonlight but I did locate onions and potatoes. Before I could search further and despite making little noise, dogs started barking. A light appeared in the first cottage followed by another further down the road. As I had obviously caused quite a disturbance I withdrew, followed the road for a few yards then made off across country.

Shortly after my fruitless venture in the hamlet gardens I came up against a railway line, my first during my walk south. It extended in a straight course to my left and right as far as one could see. Railways were a problem, subject to much sabotage they were regularly patrolled. After waiting and watching for a period it was a case of a rapid dash across and putting distance between myself and the track.

---

*Me 109 – Messerschmitt single seat fighter

The first walk in daylight

Dawn Friday 30th June, feeling sure I was well clear of the probable search area and that the Germans had more pressing problems than a wandering airman, hunger and tiredness indicated the early need for contact with the French. So far I had been fortunate with good summer weather during daylight hours. The years spent with the scouts had proved their worth in my night movements and the determination to stay free as long as possible was as strong as ever.

My practice at dawn would have been to find a suitable place to lie up for the day but convinced that the River Seine lay ahead I decided for the first time to carry on walking in daylight. Being so tired, another first was to take a Benzedrine tablet. These were only to be used if tired and in a dangerous situation; the theory being they would keep you alert and active for 24 hours. The down side however was after 24 hours you were likely to feel even more exhausted, very much an emergency measure.

At daybreak I had picked up a rough path through trees. The path wound along the top of a lightly wooded ridge and about 7 a.m. I could hear the continual noise of motor traffic. Suddenly the trees on my left thinned out and revealed below in a shallow valley a broad river with a main road on the north bank packed with German military transport heading west. The Seine at last. I had made it as hoped within my estimated six days. Uncertain if I was east or west of Rouen I continued along the path following the river downstream. (Later to find that I had struck the river a few miles east of Rouen).

In the air there was almost constant activity from Allied fighters, medium and heavy bombers including formations of Flying Fortresses.

The Seine

There were views of the road and river from time to time through the trees but the distance made it unlikely that I could be seen by the Germans. Hearing movement behind I stepped out of sight and watched a man pass along the path, his dress suggested a French workman. Giving him a short interval I rejoined the path only to walk within his vision as he sat on a log enjoying a cigarette. Whether he had seen me and was waiting I will never know. There was little to lose at this stage, he was probably a better contact in this quiet wood than elsewhere and I was almost too weary to be concerned if he was the 'right', or 'wrong' Frenchman.

Drawing level with him I gave him my best 'bon jour monsieur'. He rose and walked alongside speaking in rapid French. I had no idea what he was saying so pulled open my civilian jacket and pointed to my brevet with the words, 'Parachutist Royal Air Force'. He shook my hand, and having managed to slow down his speech, I gathered that he was taking me to meet his boss. We continued along the path; conversation was difficult but sign language did help. He claimed to speak English having once worked in a bar, but we did not make much progress other than the names of Scotch whiskies! I was really too tired to digest much of what he was saying and he did not appear unduly concerned that as we got closer to the river we were in view at intervals to the Germans on the north side of the Seine.

We eventually dropped off the ridge into a hamlet of eight small cottages either side of a rough road with a large villa at one end. It was now about 8 a.m., a beautiful warm sunny morning and there were women in all the front gardens having a neighbourly chat. As we drew near I saw a gendarme standing at the door of one cottage and thought the game was up. My escort however greeted everyone as we passed. The gendarme cast a rather curious look but we passed by and entered the villa. In the hall a full sized mirror reflected a travel stained unshaven figure; thus the odd looks from the gendarme.

In the hall we were greeted by a well built Frenchman introduced as George and I was ushered into a room. George was not his real name but that is how I knew him during my stay. To my immense relief he spoke good English. Seated at a dining room table George started what proved to be a long interrogation of my actions since baling out at Pommeréval. He was particularly interested as to how I had acquired civilian clothes. This could have been a tricky question if I had been uncertain about my new helpers but as I had no precise location of the farm my details would have harmed no one. This questioning should have been standard practice, in my two previous contacts I had been taken at face value. It was essential that helpers in the Occupied countries knew you were genuine. After this lengthy and tiring session I was shown to a bathroom and provided with shaving kit. Following a long welcome bath I returned downstairs to enjoy my first substantial meal in seven days; then I was introduced to three Frenchmen and two ladies. Conversation was difficult but made easier with George as interpreter. My new companions stressed how much the noise of Allied aircraft in the years prior to the invasion had meant; it was a message of hope. The meal was a feast after living on limited rations and one I had difficulty completing.

I never did know the name of the hamlet or its exact position other than it lay a few miles from Rouen and they were not the questions you would normally ask of your host. George had no information of other airmen picked up in the area but seemed to know that a Lancaster had been shot down near Pommeréval. After the meal I was shown to a bedroom and immediately fell asleep. On awaking I found that I had slept for 24 hours, this due to tiredness and probably the after effects of the Benzedrine tablet.

Rouen to Paris, 1st July

My uniform, flying boots, civilian jacket and trousers along with sheath knife and prismatic compass had been removed. In their place lay another set of civilian clothes and a pair of wooden soled shoes. My bomb aimer's brevet had been detached and lay on the bedside table, the brevet along with my identity discs were the only visible connection with the Royal Air Force.

Feeling much better after 24 hours' sleep, I dressed then joined George for breakfast. It was Saturday 1st July and after an action-packed week it was almost a novelty sitting down in civilised surroundings. Following breakfast, another interrogation. George wondered how I had managed to avoid trouble on the way south for it now transpired that I had walked through an area full of German troops. The Allies did not know then that Hitler still expected our main strike would be through the Pas-de-Calais and had held his reserve divisions north of the Seine. By moving at night, lying up by day and staying on high ground where possible I had avoided some problems.

By now I knew I was in the hands of the Résistance. George was a local leader and this altered my position. Our instructions were quite clear, once in the hands of the Résistance you obeyed their instructions and stopped operating on your own. When I explained my intention to stay in the Rouen area to await the Allied advance George was anything but impressed; Rouen was full of German troops. He thought that I should have headed either east or north. He advised me that all Résistance groups in the Occupied countries had received a message from London to the effect that any airmen they were holding had to be kept in as safe an area as possible pending liberation and they were not to be sent down the traditional escape routes to the south of France and over the Pyrénées.

This was hardly heartening news for aircrew in my situation. George did relieve my concern that my parents would not know that I was alive as Air Ministry would inform them only that I was missing. George confirmed that my service details had been radioed to London. On my return to London I found that the Air Ministry did not pass on such information for security reasons and as it could have raised false hopes, for the data only indicated that you were known to be alive on a certain date.

George was an engineer working or rather conscripted to work for Todt Organisation. Todt was responsible for all German military construction and employed hundreds of thousands of foreign workers in the Occupied countries and some in appalling conditions, particularly the Russian prisoners. George was currently engaged in the construction of a rocket site outside Rouen and with his Résistance involvement the site probably had an uncertain future. He produced a basic diagram of the launch site but I preferred to memorise the essential details. I still had an aversion to being shot as a spy! By the time I reached London the information was outdated, the Allies had overrun the area.

George told me that I would leave for Paris that evening as it was too dangerous to stay close to Rouen. At any other time Paris might have been a delightful prospect but during the occupation it was reputed to be one of the most perilous places in France for evaders. It also had the disadvantage of being some 90 miles to the east. The reason for the transfer was that of placing me with another Résistance group to find a safe house. It was my good fortune that George both understood and spoke English.

More disturbing news followed when George told me that I was now Paul Camus, a deaf and dumb *cimentier*. By 1944 I felt the Germans must be aware of the deaf and dumb act, but given my poor French there was little alternative. Moreover my hands had obviously never been near cement and should such close examination arise there was little hope. My present outfit of old but comfortable clothes suited my workman's role and I still retained the raincoat and haversack provided by the farmer and his wife during my walk to Rouen.

There was some discussion about my watch; it had been purchased in South Africa during my training period and not an Air Force issue, the latter would have been fatal. I did feel that probably a watch was not standard equipment for a *cimentier* but George decided that it was safe to keep it. He also insisted that I keep the bomb aimer's brevet and my identity discs despite the risk to anyone with me should I be stopped and searched. These two items stayed pinned to my underpants during my time in France.

The background to Paul Camus was that his parents had been killed in a road accident at the beginning of the war and his only living relative a grandmother who stayed in the Paris suburbs. Her home had been damaged during a RAF raid and Paul had been given permission to visit her. Contrary to some impressions, Todt Organisation workers drawn from France, Holland, Belgium were given short leaves for various reasons and also subject to transfer at brief notice.

Now as a Todt worker I was furnished with numerous papers, including letters of authority to travel to Paris, work permits, time sheets from my past work and general papers relevant to my work in the Houppeville/Rouen area. There was no time to arrange for an identity card; although we flew with a photograph designed for these mine was the wrong size. I noted that my papers stated that I was married but never did get a satisfactory answer from George particularly as I was supposed to have only one living relative! As far as George was concerned I did not look French and this view was to follow me through France. However he was not unduly concerned because of the thousands of foreign workers employed in the country.

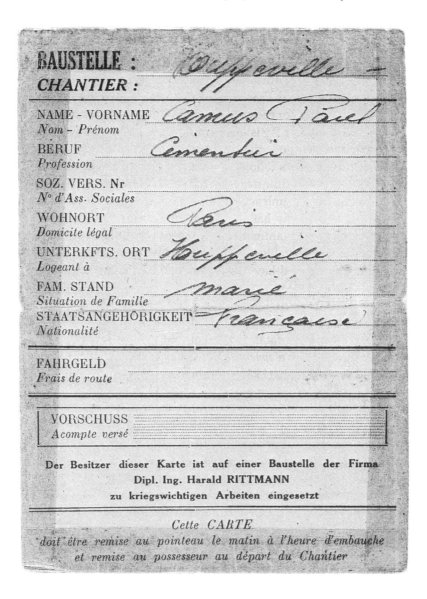

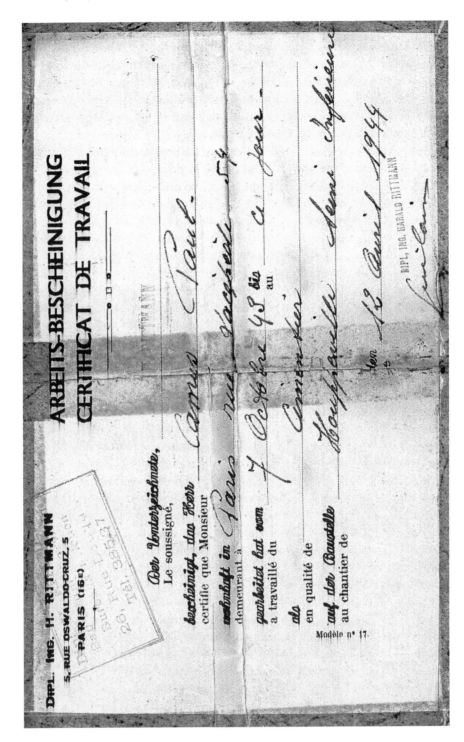

Saturday was spent quietly in the villa until just after 7 p.m. when with George and one of his friends we drove out of the hamlet in an old light Citroën 15 complete with gas bag on the roof and burner at the back, a sight that was to be a familiar one in the weeks to come. The hamlet lay a few miles from Rouen and our route took us through the outskirts of the city. As we passed through a residential district with some imposing apartment buildings a number showed heavy bomb damage. George nudged me and with a quizzical look said 'military targets'? Before I could think of a suitable reply he followed by saying 'Americans in daylight' then shrugged his shoulders. It was difficult to get the French to understand the difference in bombing techniques between the USAF in daylight and the RAF at night, although the latter were now operating both day and night. There were a considerable number of soldiers to be seen in Rouen but not as many military vehicles as I had expected. I was wondering what lay ahead on this my new venture as a member of Organisation Todt, at least I qualified as a 'foreign worker'! One followed the Résistance instructions to the letter, their lives and mine depended on such detail. It is only when I stand back from the moments of tension and realise the audacity of the French in arranging my journey to Paris with a party of Todt Organisation workers. Who would look for an airman in a Todt transport with a German escort?

It appeared that Todt workers were ferried regularly from Rouen to Paris on Saturday evenings; one of the collection venues was a bistro in Houppeville just outside the city and this is where we were bound.

In transit George gave me my instructions for Paris. It was fortunate that he had such a good command of English otherwise I may have doubted his clear but unlikely orders. I was told the transport was due at the bistro around 10 p.m. that I should board it with the other workers and that no papers were required. The lorry would drive non-stop through the night arriving in Paris between 6 and 7 on the Sunday morning stopping half way down the Champs Élysées; at that point everyone would alight. My orders were to walk forward in the direction of the Arc de Triomphe and that someone would contact me. He emphasised again that I must not talk to anyone or answer anyone on the journey.

I had never been to Paris but knew the general geography of Champs Élysées district well enough to realize that wandering down this famous avenue early one Sunday morning in Occupied Paris that someone would meet me seemed a little too fanciful to be true. This, however, was the only instruction given, plus the deaf and dumb reminder.

On arrival at the bistro I said my farewells in the car, thanking George for all his efforts on my behalf. This was my first experience of the French Résistance and one could not adequately praise their organisation and speed in the manner they operated, to say nothing of the risks taken. George took me into the bistro to meet his four companions sitting at a table and after shaking hands I sat down with them .

I had been told to act as though I knew them and in keeping with my deaf and dumb pose to watch their faces as they spoke. They were all drinking Pernod, something I recognised from my wine trade days but had never tasted. After my first glass it was clear that care would be needed if I intended to arrive in Paris in good shape. I managed to spin out my second glass for the rest of my stay in the bistro. My four new friends had a very capable look and I had the feeling that I was in safe hands.

This was my first real contact with the general public and did feel rather exposed. I assumed that most of the occupants were locals, with eight who looked possible Todt workers. It was uncomfortable just waiting, remembering to watch my companions, avoiding checking the time and taking too much interest in the bistro itself. The delay did not worry my escorts although I understood little of their conversation. With Allied fighter bombers hunting over the area, there was every reason to expect delays in road movements, but it still made for an uneasy two hours maintaining my act and ignoring all other activities.

The transport arrived about 10 p.m. in the form of a German army troop carrier with the typical high clearance of the British army personnel lorries. With two rough bench type seats either side it was already three quarters full with most standing. The escort comprised three *Wehrmacht* soldiers including the driver.

My instructions were to wait until the Todt Organisation workers rose to leave and then join them as they walked out. In terms of dress I did not feel out of place but did notice that I was younger than most. My companions left me at the bistro entrance, the lorry tailboard had been lowered and I was given a hand up by one of the soldiers. The irony of that gesture, a German giving me a helping hand on my way to Paris has stayed with me over the years. Once on board I edged forward until able to grasp a roof spar, the canvas roof no doubt had long since disappeared. The lorry was now full and made for very cramped conditions but the dark did help to make it more difficult for anyone to talk to you.

As we drove out of Houppeville low cloud settled with a light drizzle and although not pleasant in the rain it was something of a blessing for the road from Rouen to Paris was littered with burnt out vehicles as the result of fighter rocket and cannon fire. It proved a tiring business standing and hanging on to the roof spar but it did give me the chance to appear to be half asleep. On two occasions during the early part of the journey comments were made in my direction. I shrugged my shoulders hoping that would satisfy them; they must have thought I was very unsociable. As daylight broke an oldish man at my side nudged me and pointed to a field with the word, 'Spitfire'. There close to the road lay a Mustang that had made a good belly landing and intact enough to clearly identify. I automatically replied, no *'Mustang'. Fortunately there was no reaction but it emphasised how easily you could be caught unawares by a simple question whilst acting deaf and dumb and a reminder that my tired state was no excuse.

Paris, 2nd July

We entered Paris just before 7 a.m. The rain had stopped, it was overcast and chilly in damp clothes. Paris seemed drab and dingy in the early morning light but the very fact of arriving in the city for me created great interest. At that hour there were few signs of life, probably typical for a Sunday morning either French or German. I had expected to see more German troops.

The lorry stopped in the Champs Élysées, the tailboard was lowered and the same German soldier who had assisted me aboard in Houppeville gave me a hand down. Paris a city of world renown but at my age not one I had expectations of visiting. Eight days after dropping into Occupied France I presented a rather cold damp figure standing in the centre of the Capital, a place hardly noted for its welcome to Allied airmen. I could safely say that it was not my most comfortable day in France.

With little idea of what would develop and some misgivings about my instructions I set off towards the Arc de Triomphe hoping I looked the part as a workman. With so few people around I felt somewhat conspicuous even allowing for the fact there were so few Germans in sight. It was a question of trying to look natural but at the same time being only too aware of the imposing surroundings. Despite the irony of an Allied airman wandering in the most famous avenue in Occupied France, one could only admire the logic and the almost simple way the Résistance introduced me to Paris, 'safe' in the hands of a German escort yet I had posed a serious risk to all on the lorry. My immediate concern was what action to take if my contact did not appear before reaching the Arc de Triomphe, hardly the place for a workman to loiter.

A short distance from the lorry I was tapped on the shoulder and a

---

*Known as the P 51 by the USAAF and Mustang by the RAF, a long range single seat fighter

Frenchman just said, 'Follow me'. I recognised him as having travelled with me and found later that two had made the journey to ensure that no one spoke to me and that I kept my dumb stance. I discovered the matter of following someone was quite an art and one to give me problems during the ensuing weeks. My contact never looked round and trying to hold a reasonable gap and a natural attitude was never easy. The French were to despair of me in two ways; they said I did not look French and that I did not walk like the French!; the latter comment probably due to the fact that I had always been a very fast walker. The former did not cause undue worry because of the large number of foreign workers (thanks to Organisation Todt) in France.

After a week of walking at night only and seeing little of the countryside this was an entirely new experience. I made a point of avoiding street names and trying to remember prominent buildings on the basis that if picked up I would have had little information to impart. Everything around me created interest but my priority that of keeping my contact in sight; he eventually stopped outside a large villa and beckoned me forward. We walked into the villa to be introduced to a lady. The lady spoke a little English and told me that I would be staying the night.

After breakfast my escort wished me well and took his leave. From the lady's limited English and my poor French I gathered that I would be passed on to another Résistance group and hidden in the Paris area. She did stress that conditions were difficult and dangerous and that I might be moved without warning. After a rest the lady returned in the afternoon and asked if I would like a lady companion for the night, a language misunderstanding I thought, until it dawned that the villa was probably a house for the 'ladies of the night'. *Scouting for Boys* had not covered this aspect! I hoped that I had not offended my host by declining as politely as my French permitted. She smiled and shrugged her shoulders as I indicated that after a sleepless night's journey, a rest was my greatest need. It seemed that I had more than Germans to concern me, the 'auld alliance' may have meant more than I thought!

During the next few days there were visits to three different groups or rather their leaders and after the usual interrogation my future was discussed. My lack of French restricted some safe house opportunities and such interviews were difficult given the language problems on both sides. The venues for these meetings were quite varied, including one almost hilarious episode in a laundry where I would assist in the rear of the building and occupy the flat above. As my French almost reduced the ladies to tears the idea was fortunately dropped. On an another occasion I was interviewed by two young men standing in front of a Gendarmerie in a Paris suburb,

French logic again in the sense that the last place you would expect to find an Allied airman would be in front of a police station.

My clothes seemed to be effective in as much they attracted no unusual attention; the problem remained that of following contacts both male and female. It was necessary to use the metro on two occasions and here I was particularly keen to keep my helpers in sight. The Metro was dangerous in that it was watched by the Gestapo and I had been told to be careful when joining and leaving the Metro. In concentrating on my contacts I may have overlooked the fact that I was acquiring information about the Résistance that would have been of great interest to the Gestapo and that they had some disturbing ways of extracting such details.

The fifth day brought two separate interrogations at different venues in the search for a safe house. That evening I was transferred to a flat in the Rue des Panoyaux in the Menilmontant district, my hosts on this occasion Msr George and Madame Mauricette Guilani. The Guilanis, a young couple in their late twenties with a child just over a year old, Mauricette spoke a little English, her husband none. The one fear common to all evaders was the danger they caused to their helpers and I found it a great embarrassment that I should put at risk such a young family. On their part there was no resentment of the obvious perils, they explained that it was their duty to help me, it meant something they could do against the Germans, and the other point, that it was their duty to return me to 'Angleterre to fight again'! The family did not appear to be well off, they would not however accept any of the francs I carried; no one during my stay in France would accept the money we flew with; the usual excuse, the notes were too clean.

Food was very scarce throughout Paris; food eaten in the flat was always shared equally no matter how little. The Guilani flat occupied part of the third floor in a five storey apartment block. Although they knew my name I did not know their surnames until after the war when Mauricette wrote to the Air Ministry with a letter to be forwarded.

Conditions in Paris were deteriorating rapidly following the invasion in Normandy, the food position, never good during the occupation was now much worse. The situation as to whether or not Paris would be declared an open city caused great concern. During my stay in Paris I could get little reliable information about the battle in Normandy. Rumours were rife and my language problem did not help but it was clear that no early breakout from the Normandy bridgeheads had been achieved.

The Guilani family faced a constant food shortage; our main meal, lunch, we took at a bistro a short distance from the flat, usually bread, soup and wine. Wine of some sort always seemed to be available. I was never sure what I ate but everything had to be consumed, in my case a fastidious eater was soon converted. The bistro visits emphasised the strange situation and danger to the Guilani family sitting with a RAF evader in such public surroundings; perhaps there is something in the saying 'lost in a crowd'. The other occupants I assumed were locals with the exception of the odd table of German soldiers; these were either on the young side or fairly old, certainly not first line troops. Their presence did little to put my mind at rest. I could only think that it was the food problem that made the family take these risks in public. This was the only period whilst in Paris that I walked with my helpers on our daily visit to the bistro.

Conversation with the family was not easy but we made some progress; they showed considerable interest in my home life and were surprised to find that I was in the wine trade. The fact of being Scottish created an even friendlier atmosphere, an attitude found with many helpers. One question they raised and to be repeated often during my stay in France was, 'What did the English think of the French?'. They felt that they had let us down in 1940 and their politicians were responsible for the collapse; in this respect they were quite correct. One could only assure them that we were all now fighting a common cause.

After returning from lunch on the second day we heard the screech of tyres in the street below and George shouted, 'Allemand' (Germans). He dashed down the hallway to open the front door then returned to move me to the bedroom where I was placed on the end of the bed and given a book to read. The layout of the flat meant that anyone standing at the front door and looking down the hall would see the area of the bedroom where I sat supposedly reading.

The sound of boots on the stone stairs could be heard as the soldiers raced up the five floors, as I sat on the bed a soldier stopped at the open front door, glanced down the hall, could obviously see me then walked on. The Germans withdrew fairly quickly; the family had no idea why the raid had taken place and did not think that it had anything to do with me. If they were seriously concerned they did not show it.

Two days later at a similar time in the afternoon there was another raid; the same procedure was followed, the front door left wide open and on this occasion Mauricette and baby sat alongside me on the bed. As the troops worked their way up through the five floors a German NCO paused at the door then moved to the floor above. Like the first intrusion no one appeared to have been detained.

Two more days passed, now my sixth in the flat when we were all caught unexpectedly with a swoop at 5 a.m. on the Sunday morning. We heard the noise of soldiers in the courtyard and the different landings in the block. There was no time to be wasted, I was placed behind the bed and a blanket thrown over me. George had again opened the front door, his wife and baby sitting at the foot of the bed. I could not witness this visit but a soldier walked down the hall to the bedroom door, glanced round the room and walked away without speaking.

Three raids in six days, the Germans were obviously looking for someone or something, thus the danger of being picked up on the wrong sort of sweep. I doubt if they were looking for an Allied airman but given my age they would surely have asked for papers, and whatever else the Germans may have been they were not stupid.

A letter from the Guilani family with whom in July 1944 I spent a week in their 'safe house'.

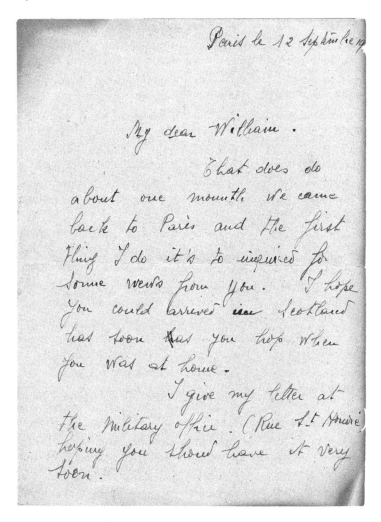

The reasoning behind the opening of the flat front door on each raid was the assumption that with large numbers of soldiers rushing through each floor landing, the open door would suggest the flat was being searched. A tenuous line of thought and one we were lucky to get away with. That final raid was also to be my last day in the flat, I was moved the next morning.

The week spent with this family had made a great impression on me and illustrated how the ordinary men and women in France were prepared to risk their lives for unknown Allied airmen, in this instance all the more poignant as they had a young baby. The hatred of the Germans and all they stood for ran deep; the act of helping me was one of the ways they could strike back. All evaders carried a heavy responsibility, a wrong move or

My husband send you all his best wishes and think I could see you again in Paris or other where very soon.

In Paris, we are all happy to see the English soldiers

& I hope you keep a good "souvenir" from us, when you past near Rouen "incognito" — Everybody send you and the best wishes, and received from your French fried her best kinds regards.

Yours

Marinette Giuliani

P.S. I hope you could handerstand my bad English

word could have disastrous consequences and the helpers themselves were at risk from betrayal. I left the Guillanis hoping that my poor French conveyed my genuine gratitude for all they had risked. They no doubt shared my relief in one sense at being moved on.

My new contact guided me to a flat near Orly airport. This time the interview was carried out by three Frenchmen and proved to be the most testing yet. Apart from describing what had happened to me over the past fortnight they were keen to establish details of my previous bombing operations. As one moved to different helpers or groups you only gave an outline of your movements in France and no specific details or names, nor did you provide operational information other than comments like, 'Bombed targets in Germany'. By this time I possessed considerable data relating to helpers and could expect problems if picked up by the Germans so great care was necessary. I was beginning to doubt the credentials of my interviewers and things were rather tense until I was asked about my home in Edinburgh. At the mention of this city it turned out that one member had been there and an exchange of well known localities satisfied them. The contact I had followed to the flat said it was used by French Intelligence,* I doubted if they would have any interest in a wandering airman; he did add that if they had not been satisfied I would have been shot. This highlighted the problem of Germans disguised in RAF uniform to trap the Résistance groups. The next three days were spent in two different flats near Orly airport. With my inadequate French it was difficult to find out what was going on other than my helpers were becoming very concerned at the deteriorating situation in Paris. The hot summer weather continued and it was a tedious, tiring wait each day for information about my future.

On the 12th July I followed a courier on foot and by Metro back into the centre of Paris arriving at a shipping office in the Rue Chopin, the area between the River Seine and the Bois-de-Boulogne. Here I was introduced to a M. Castelman, his student son and his secretary Jacqueline Tibbatts an attractive young lady, all three fluent in English. M. Castelman stated that the City had become too dangerous and I was being transferred to Ermont, a village some seven miles north on the Paris to Pontoise Road. Jacqueline would be responsible for my safety and provide my instructions. Few

---

*Many years after the war, a young lady management trainee joined my department. She had been introduced by Colonel Buckmaster of SOE fame, and had been instructed to pass on his compliments to me with the message that I would not know or remember him but that our paths had crossed. I could not help wondering if that Paris meeting had any connection.

Jacqueline Tibbats with Msr Castelman on left and Msr Bataille.
This was my last venue in Paris on 12th July 1944, the office of the
shipper in the Rue Chopin.

evaders had such a charming guardian, she was a Résistance courier and had already served three months in the notorious Fresnes prison in Paris for anti-German activities. Her strong views were such you felt they could lead her into danger. I was told that my deaf and dumb pose was finished and in future to use French only; my conversations were going to be very limited! Ermont would be my home until liberation.

My spell in Paris had ended and although there had been anxious moments, I realised why the Capital earned the reputation as a most dangerous place for evaders. It was always a question of who could be trusted in a congested city; there were too many eyes and ears. I had received assistance from people at various levels of society all at risk of their lives. I could not say that I became used to walking the same streets as the Germans but it was a fact of life and the stress lay in trying to maintain a natural attitude and hopefully blend in with the locals. It was but a brief insight to conditions under German occupation and underlined the reasons why we were at war. My impression of Paris was that of a tired population where trust in each other had been badly shaken and who now desperately awaited the arrival of the Allied forces and so their freedom. I could only hope these expectations would soon be realised. Ermont for me might not be any safer but it did hold promise as my last 'safe house'.

Departure from Paris

In the afternoon I left the shipping office as a pillion passenger on Castelman's son's motor bike, my first such journey and one never to be forgotten. The main crossroads in Paris were manned by German patrols and as we sped through them I would be nudged along with the shout of 'Boche' and I did feel that my back was rather exposed. This hair-raising journey finished at his parents' home in the suburbs to a great welcome from his mother and to find a cycle waiting for me.

Jacqueline arrived in the early evening and after a meal we set off for Ermont. After spending anxious moments following my contacts around Paris it was both a change and a pleasure to be cycling alongside Jacqueline to a new destination.

The journey led through the suburbs, then a mixture of more open housing and rural areas providing interesting and new sights. We avoided the main Paris to Pontoise road and thus did not encounter too many Germans; those we did pass did not appear to be interested in two cyclists on a warm July evening. Despite little traffic there were few opportunities for safe conversation apart from Jacqueline giving instructions at intervals.

Jacqueline Tibbats, Ermont 1944.
A very courageous lady, my 'guardian', July/August 1944.

Ermont, the safe house, 12th July

On arrival in Ermont I found that my home was to be the top flat in a traditional solid stone building in the Rue Berthelot; the flat had the usual full length windows typical throughout France. The owners had moved to the South of France for safety as the block was sited next to a railway junction and station; communications at this period of the war were being blasted by Allied bombers all over the Occupied countries and in particular, France.

We visited first the flat belonging to Jacqueline on the ground floor where she produced some of her brother's clothes, which fortunately proved a good fit. Her brother 'Bob' had managed to reach England and she understood that he was serving with the Free French Navy. My workman style clothes had now been replaced, thanks to Bob, by a more appropriate garb. I was horrified to find that her bedroom was adorned with photographs of Churchill and our Royal Family, most extracted from magazines; this did seem to be stretching her luck following her earlier brush with the Gestapo.

While she prepared a meal, she outlined the procedure to be followed at Ermont during the time she would be in Paris. For the benefit of the villagers I was to be known as a cousin of the flat owners, asked to look after the property in their absence. My instructions were to stay indoors during the day until Jacqueline returned in the evening, to stay away from windows, to keep as quiet as possible, socks only to be worn during the day and no radio to be used until she joined me, usually about 6 o'clock at night.

Following the meal I was introduced to her mother who occupied the opposite ground floor flat. Mdme Tibbatts, a charming lady presently working as a nurse, was a Hollander who had married an English soldier from the First World War and her husband was presently interned in a civilian camp outside Paris. This background explained Jacqueline's almost fluent English. It was agreed that her mother would not be involved in my stay in the flat; for her safety the less she knew the better and I had no further contact until Ermont was liberated.

We then moved up to the top flat. It proved to be well appointed and after showing me the layout and items that I would need Jacqueline left saying friends might be joining me shortly. During the tour of the apartment I realised that in one respect it was a trap should the block ever be raided, there was no hiding place inside and no access to the roof from the interior. The roof overhang was such that only a gymnast could swing out, up and over the edge. That ruled me out; the RAF trained us how to fall, but not from the fourth floor!

So began my wait in Ermont; Jacqueline soon returned with three friends, all students involved with Résistance activities. They were Pierre Galy, his sister Hélène and her fiance Jean Collin. (Jean and Hélène married after the war.) Jean had been ordered to report for work with Todt Organisation and had moved out of the family home, so in effect he was 'wanted'. Along with Jacqueline these three delightful and brave characters were to be my constant companions.

Pierre was about my size and of a rather serious and studious nature, Jean the tallest with a suggestion of an adventurous approach and Hélène was a charming petite, elegant young lady with a delightful discerning attitude; an intelligent wonderful trio with whom I was to share my remaining weeks in France. They seemed to accept the risks of being associated with me as a matter of course, despite the penalty of death at the hands of the Gestapo. I was in contact with them through Jacqueline almost every day. Conversation with Pierre and Jean was rather difficult but it was surprising how much we could convey. Hélène understood much of my speech but was unable to respond. Jacqueline was a striking, vivacious lady with a great sense of fun and a no nonsense approach that at times could have meant trouble in Occupied France. They all appreciated the dangers of dealing with the Germans, and she was of course my invaluable interpreter.

Having been introduced, they listened to my story translated by Jacqueline and after hearing the BBC news they departed saying they would join me the next day. This was the first time I had heard the BBC since arriving in France and it was a welcome sound even if it did emphasise my isolated position over the Channel. The words, 'Ici Londres' had a magic touch to the French, it was the constant reminder that they had not been forgotten. The strangely worded code messages were directed at those groups involved in sabotage and reconnaissance but also reflected the ongoing activities of the underground movement.

Pierre provided me with a map of France and with coloured pins I maintained an outline of the battle fronts as indicated on the BBC news, this often at variance with the German controlled radio broadcasts.

My Ermont friends were very interested in wartime life in Britain and our bombing campaign in Germany, in respect of the latter they had little reliable information. The French were particularly impressed by the RAF precision raids on the Renault factory at *Billancourt and the Trappes railway yards both in the Paris environs where virtually no bombs fell outside the target areas and there were few casualties. There seemed to be a general

---

*Billancourt attacked 3/4th March 1942 and Trappes 6/7th March 1944.

sympathetic resignation to our need to attack targets in France and the other Occupied countries.

To-date the French had insisted that I retain my brevet and identity discs despite the obvious danger to anyone caught with me. I raised this matter again with Jacqueline with the response that my poor French and out of date papers would enable the Germans to quickly establish my true identity. She felt that I would be more likely treated as a prisoner of war rather than a 'saboteur'; this was a generous interpretation considering that anyone with me would face certain death. The longer I stayed in France and the more contacts made, increased the danger to my helpers. When my new friends left, Jacqueline took me on another tour of the flat giving various instructions and then tried to improve my French, a major problem for anyone!

Once we were on our own Jacqueline said she would be moving into the other bedroom. Given that there was no alternative exit I thought this an unnecessary risk should the Germans pay a call, however she was not to be persuaded otherwise. With authority to look after the flat she wished to be on hand to deal with any problems. Living under the same roof we developed a close relationship, there were no language difficulties and thus no misunderstanding; her instructions were always clear as to the do's and don'ts both inside and outside the flat.

In Paris my movements had been restricted to visiting different Résistance contacts and apart from the week going to the bistro for lunch, I was now entering a period when daily exposure would be routine. Many evaders for very good reasons were kept hidden away; my helpers thought I should get as much exercise as possible subject to local German activity. This entailed evening walks around the village with longer journeys at the weekends. There were German patrols in the village itself but the main military movement took place on the Paris–Pontoise road at the edge of the village.

Food was a constant problem and although I had been a fussy eater before the war, now it was a case of being grateful for anything that your hosts served, particularly when everything was equally shared. During my stay in Ermont I was taken to a few trusted houses and clearly items that had been hidden away for a special occasion were produced for my benefit. On one visit a packet of tea kept since the fall of France was opened. In view of their shortages it was embarrassing that I could only offer them danger in return. Here as in Paris no one would accept my francs. With no knowledge of French rural towns and villages for comparison, I can only describe Ermont as a large village with a range of well-built houses and apartment blocks built around the railway station and junction.

The hot summer continued and now clear of Paris where few Allied aircraft were heard it was a return to almost constant air traffic; Allied bombers both day and night, now Bomber Command Lancasters were a regular sight in daylight along with the Flying Fortresses. The long straight stretch of railway line from the north to Ermont station attracted the attention of our fighter-bombers and I was witness to some spectacular actions against such rolling stock that ventured out in daylight; the Spitfire and Mustang fighter attacks were completely successful.

My right shoulder had become rather stiff and painful, this was the shoulder that had taken the full impact when baling out with only one harness strap attached. At the end of the first week in Ermont a doctor came to see me, a visit organised unbeknown to me by Jacqueline and her mother. I was told that the injury needed hospital treatment but would have to wait until my return to the United Kingdom.

The first fortnight passed quietly in the summer heat, although the need for silence and minimum movement made for long tedious hours during the day. There were a number of books in the flat but really beyond my limited French. The only English book was *Three Men in a Boat* which was certainly read from cover to cover. The long verandah style windows meant that I had good vision in most directions from well back in the room without being exposed and situated on the top floor I could not be overlooked. The familiar noise from Allied aircraft emphasised the situation of being so close and yet so far from safety.

The presence of a heavy anti-aircraft battery to the north of the village, part of the outer perimeter defences of Paris, was a constant reminder of the danger to Allied planes; these heavy batteries were accurate and a hint that the Germans were not going to be easily moved. This particular battery was to prove fatal to two Lancasters, if not the crews on the 6th and 8th of August.

On most evenings after Jacqueline's return from Paris we would be joined by Pierre, Jean and Hélène and walk through the village. Any meetings with the locals were kept brief, usually an exchange of the normal courtesies of the day. My escorts were quite happy for me to return such greetings but any questions directed at me were answered by one of the three. Jacqueline did try to improve my French without much success, she was also keen that I point out any mistakes in her English grammar. Jean would say tongue in cheek, that if I wished to speak properly I should spend six months with a French lady! It did have a certain appeal. Jacqueline and I would converse in English in the flat to improve her grammar but that did little for my French. Outside we would sometimes use English where and when it was safe to do so, the latter almost had serious consequences as will be noted later.

Arrangements had been made for a hairdresser to visit the flat but nothing could be done about the identity card; the problem was finding a photographer they could trust. By now one had some idea of the problems faced by the peoples in the Occupied countries under the strict rules and penalties enforced by the Germans. Apart from the obvious danger from the Gestapo and their means of extracting information, the Vichy Milice were held in greater fear. The Vichy Milice, a para-military police French force, worked closely with the Gestapo; one could possibly fool the Germans but not the Milice, such men were the real traitors in France.

Food remained a problem although conditions were better in Ermont than experienced in Paris; Jacqueline always seemed to be able to provide something and to have a knack of adding flavour to very basic ingredients.

As the days passed into August with the daily evening stroll round Ermont and cycle visits at the weekends to trusted families continued, the feeling of being accepted as part of the village life did not remove my impression of being over exposed. This danger was apparent about three weeks after my arrival in the village when leaving the flat one evening with Jacqueline a lady dashed out after me, grasped my hand with the words, 'I want to meet the parachutist Anglais'. I said nothing but recognised her as the lady who lived in the flat below me. Jacqueline dealt with her and when we moved away explained that the neighbour had seen me on numerous occasions and was quite convinced that I was not 'the cousin', did not look French, did not walk like the French (that walk again) and was certain that I was a parachutist.

With my movements around Ermont there must have been many who were dubious about this so called cousin, and it is to their lasting credit that I was never betrayed. The Germans were becoming increasingly trigger happy and, if I had been picked up, villagers other than my immediate helpers could have been at risk.

Jacqueline was keen that we walked arm-in-arm when practical out in Ermont as part of my cover, and it supported the local rumour that I was her fiance; certainly no hardship with two such charming ladies as Jacqueline and Hélène, but I was mindful that it increased the risk to them both and that we lived in an atmosphere of never knowing whom you could trust.

It seemed impossible to shake off the double-life feeling moving about in Occupied France; always trying to blend in with the local community and yet being such a danger to those with you. With the war situation improving there was the risk that familiarity would bring its own problems.

On most Sunday mornings I would join my four companions and cycle to the nearest town, Enghien-les-Bains. Once there we made our way to a man-made lake in the town centre where we cycled round the lake two or

These were the only photographs of Bill Knaggs during the occupation.

With Jacqueline Tibbats at Bouffèment 6th August 1944.

Below:
Taken during a visit to a family at Bouffèment 6th August 1944.
Left to right: Jacqueline Tibbats, Bill Knaggs. (Bouffèment, a village a few miles from Ermont.)

three times before resting on the lake shore, a popular local rendezvous. The practice itself might not have been unusual but for the fact that the casino on the lake-side now housed the Gestapo as the area headquarters. It did seem unnecessary to cycle pass the building during our circuits of the lake; when I raised the matter the attitude was that the Germans would get used to seeing us together. I was never convinced, the word together hardly a safety factor for my helpers given Jean was 'wanted' and I was an evader.

This approach to risk arose during a visit in August to the Galy home on the outskirts of Ermont. I had been invited for a meal and to meet the family and their relatives one Sunday afternoon. There were nine at the table, I had been introduced as Jacqueline's friend Paul Camus and played little part in the conversation. When we were having coffee (or what passed for coffee) Pierre Galy's father suddenly announced that I was an 'avaiteur Anglais'. A middle aged man opposite me almost dropped his cup and departed soon after. He was a cousin but I did feel in the circumstances the Galy family should have chosen their guests with greater care, the cousin no doubt thought the same.

German troops were a regular sight in the village and also made use of the railway station. During July there was continual military traffic moving north from Paris towards Pontoise at night. Starting in August the military withdrawal took place both day and night and now attracted attention from Allied fighter aircraft.

The only photographs taken of me during the Occupation were with some close friends of Jacqueline at Bouffèment where there was a family she insisted I meet. On the 6th August we cycled a few miles to the village. I arrived to a great welcome and spent the afternoon with them. With Jacqueline as translator, they had many questions about the war and also repeated a point taken up with me at other venues, that the noise and sight of Allied bombers during the early days of occupation gave them hope when all seemed lost and that they had not been abandoned. The importance of this moral support was probably not appreciated by the Allies at the time. One of the constant dangers of these cycle trips was the risk of German patrols setting up check points to examine papers; mine were now out of date.

Updating the map provided by Pierre showing the battle fronts based on the BBC evening broadcasts just added to tedious long hours of waiting throughout the day inasmuch they showed little movement from the Allies in Normandy. Caen was taken on the 8th August and now with action on all fronts the Allies landed in the South of France on the 15th August and I could now give heartening news to my friends.

This monument was erected by the people of Ermont after liberation in memory of the crews of two Lancasters shot down by anti-aircraft fire over the village on the 6th and 8th August 1944.

One unusual trip was taken on a Sunday from Ermont when, with my four companions, we cycled to a well known beauty spot and viewing point on a wooded hill north of the village. They wanted me to see the delightful view of the Seine valley. As we sat on the hillside in the warm sun admiring the view and watching numerous French couples and small groups of German soldiers walking leisurely on the hill the peaceful scene was at odds with the reality of sitting amidst enemy forces.

A few French girls were escorted by Germans much to the anger of my friends. Given the panoramic scene one could appreciate how popular this spot must have been and the distaste felt at seeing Germans wandering on the hill.

On the 8th August a Lancaster was hit by flak from the AA battery just outside the village. I had watched the formation approaching; it was a clear, brilliant summer afternoon. As fire spread the crew baled out. I counted seven parachutes and although they were falling close to Ermont there was nothing I could do.

To my surprise about an hour later there was a knock on the door (we had a prearranged signal knock). On opening I was faced with a tall young man in civilian dress and accompanied by a member of the local Résistance whom I knew by sight. He introduced the *stranger as F/Lt. Hughes, the pilot of the Lancaster I had just seen shot down. We shook hands then he was on his way. The Frenchman had insisted that he meet the other parachutist in Ermont! I found out later that they had both cycled through the cordon of German troops closing in on the village to search for the crew; there was no news of the other survivors. It illustrated again the rapid response and risks the French were prepared to take in assisting our airmen.

With improving reports from the battle fronts, there was an air of expectation in the village and with my helpers to the extent I felt over confidence could lead to carelessness.

Early one Sunday morning en route to join the Galy family, Jacqueline and I were passing the railway station; with no one in sight and in the centre of the road we were conversing in English. Ermont, a typical rural station had no platform but a series of bench seats backed by hedges, as we walked I had a feeling that we were not alone and turning round slowly saw a German soldier who had been hidden by the hedge watching us with a puzzled look. Jacqueline took my arm as we walked slowly to the next corner then moved very rapidly. The soldier may not have heard us clearly but it was a stern reminder of the wartime adage 'careless talk costs

---

*I had no doubt the 'stranger' was the pilot but was uncertain that his name was Hughes

lives'. We arrived at the Galy home in the Rue du Maréchal-Joffre without further incident.

By the 20th August there was a great feeling of tension and expectation; Jacqueline could no longer travel safely to Paris with the German retreat now in full flow; there were rumours of the Allies close to Paris; and in Paris itself still no certainty that it would be declared an open city. I was never privy to the local Résistance group activities, but was asked by one member to explain the actions of a Browning machine gun; they had received a small supply of these weapons. The gun was brought round to the flat; I knew the gun from my short spell with the Home Guard in Edinburgh. Armed members of the group were now seen from time to time in the village.

There was a deceptive air of confidence with the thought of early liberation and once again our guard dropped. Jacqueline had somehow taken delivery of a small cask of Banyuls red wine; it was held in the cellars under the flats. On the 21st August I was asked to join Pierre and Jean in the cellar to bottle the wine; they had an assortment of bottles in various shapes and sizes. We commenced to bottle, the system being that you filled the bottle to the top of the neck then drank off enough wine to make room for the cork which was dealt with by a hand corking machine. The inevitable result, three very happy characters with Pierre and Jean insisting on singing English songs. These sounds would have drifted out through the gratings on to the street. Fortunately Jacqueline arrived with some old fashioned French words to restore order, but it was a symptom of the prevailing mood and something that would not have happened weeks earlier.

The next day there was a tragic incident in the village square. A local ambulance was stopped by a German patrol, an NCO and a soldier. They ordered the driver and his companion to open the rear doors and on finding the vehicle full of bread the NCO killed them with his machine pistol. There seemed no reason for this atrocity other than the ambulance was not used for its normal purpose; the Germans were quite trigger happy at this stage in the retreat from Paris. With the acute food shortage the ambulance was possibly one of the few transports likely to get through.

On the same day there was sad news from Paris, M. Castelman's son who had taken me out of Paris on his motor cycle had been killed. He had attended a Résistance meeting in a cellar, the Gestapo must have been alerted, grenades were rolled into the cellar and all were killed.

We heard on the 22nd August that the heavy anti aircraft batteries north of Ermont were pulling out, although it was becoming difficult to establish fact from rumour but the main road from Paris to Pontoise carried a continuous stream of military vehicles and ordnance. This proved too tempting a target for the local Résistance groups who were now openly carrying arms. They struck at the German convoys on the 23rd. This was an ill timed venture with the Allies so close; the French were only lightly armed and no match for the Germans. The locals suffered many casualties, the Germans deployed some troops and limited street fighting took place. They were concerned with the armed Résistance only and did not carry out a search of buildings.

From my vantage point I had a view of some of the fighting and it was during this skirmish that I saw a wounded German soldier lying in the road. When I asked Jacqueline why the French didn't move him or help him, she shrugged her shoulders with the comment he is German, leave him. This attitude seemed heartless, but even with my short spell in occupied territory, I could understand the depth of feeling. An appreciation of this situation is almost impossible to convey in the United Kingdom, a country that has not known occupation by an enemy. The German soldier was eventually recovered by his own troops.

Liberation

Late in the evening of the 23rd August shells were being fired over the village in the direction of the retreating Germans. It was our first indication that Allied troops were close; luckily none fell in the village. Another new experience, I had never been under shell fire before.

On the 25th August, Paris was liberated. It meant so much to the French after years of occupation. Their joy was such that it is almost impossible to describe; treasured bottles that had been hidden were suddenly produced and shared.

Just after daybreak on the 26th I was asked to go to the village square as a jeep had arrived. I assumed I had misinterpreted the message as it seemed unlikely, but it was a jeep with two Canadian officers. They were trying to make contact with the Germans and wanted details of our last sightings. Having told them the enemy left two hours earlier they drove off down the same road. I did not rate their chances of survival too high but they returned late that night. They explained that they could not help me but that I could expect to see General Patton's armour within three days. With that cheering information the jeep headed back in the direction of Paris.

Early on the morning of 29th August we were awakened by the sound of tanks. Jacqueline and I dashed down to the centre of Ermont to be met by a slow moving armoured column, a welcome and impressive sight, tanks and carriers as far as the eye could see, to say nothing of a small communications aircraft overhead. The whole of Ermont had turned out to give the Americans a tremendous welcome.

I jumped aboard a tank and introduced myself to the commander, an American Lieutenant, and gave him my details. It was obvious I was not the first airman he had picked up on his journey from the South of France and was familiar with the situation. After my explanation his first words were, 'Come with us we are chasing Jerry'. The idea of continuing the war in a tank had no appeal at all! Apart from anything else, I could not abandon my helpers like that. Having turned down his offer of a 'lift', I was told that my service details would be sent by radio to Paris when the column stopped in the evening and that I would have to report to the Hotel Meurice within three days otherwise they would be looking for me. This famous hotel was now Allied Group Intelligence HQ; the Meurice had been the former German Commandant General's Paris headquarters during the Occupation.

I rejoined Jacqueline and we made our way to the Galy home to a memorable celebration; their joy and relief at liberation was indescribable. My experience was but a glimpse of their years of humiliation and suffering. Much wine flowed and luxuries tucked away for years for this occasion now appeared. They were loath to let us leave but it was necessary to return to Rue Berthelot, now free to meet Jacqueline's mother and enjoy yet another celebration.

It was established that the route back to Paris was not officially safe as the Germans had left snipers to the north of the city and we were advised to wait. Despite this warning Jacqueline wished to see her father, so the next day we cycled to his internment camp outside Paris. He could not be released immediately as certain formalities had to be completed and he expected to be home within a week. The camp of course was open and the inmates free to move about. Like most of the internees he had suffered from food shortages but seemed reasonably fit. I think he was proud of Jacqueline's actions; the family had been able to visit him during his internment and take food parcels.

A free man again thanks initially to the French and finally General Patton's armoured division, my freedom the result of the courage and enterprise shown by the ordinary men and women of France and the Résistance movement.

A very special relationship had built up during the weeks spent with Jacqueline, Pierre, Hélène and Jean. There is a bond that unites people sharing danger; this was very true of RAF bomber crews, all interdependent on one another. The same applied to my four helpers; we had grown very close. Sharing a flat with Jacqueline brought a particular friendship. On my arrival in Ermont and our exchange of personal information, I had told her that I was engaged. This engagement proved the barrier that prevented us becoming intimate in the way the word is used today, a barrier that was a constant temptation, she was a vivacious lady in every sense, someone to be treasured and never forgotten.

It was time to return to duty, although there was a feeling that it would never be the same without my old crew. I had carried out the Air Force instructions i.e. 'you are expected to return to base, preferably with your aircraft' a short phrase but not always easy to carry out. Despite all the help received, good luck played a major part; dropping into France in a very hot summer had solved some possible problems, the same journey in winter could have been another tale.

Snipers were still active outside Paris but on the 2nd September after farewells to the Galy family and Madame Tibbatts the four friends who had risked so much took me back to Paris. It was a beautiful sunny day as we cycled, a fitting day to enter a liberated city and a safer journey than my exit some weeks earlier on a motor cycle. During our ride there was an exchange of fire in the suburbs as the Résistance flushed out German snipers. It was an exhilarating way to return on my first step home.

Paris – a free city, 2nd September 1944

On arrival in the city centre I was given a whirlwind tour of those famous landmarks that my friends considered a must for any visitor to Paris. During this hectic sight seeing trip I saw very few Allied troops but was surprised to meet two American *Thunderbolt pilots who had managed to get leave within five days of the liberation of the city, and asked them to take some group photographs. It was a fascinating day and what a dramatic difference after my spell in Occupied Paris.

After the long eventful day we returned to the Hotel Meurice there to say our emotional farewells. These brave friends had risked all; the war still continued and no one could be certain of the future. I was not to know that I would never see Jacqueline again; happily I was to maintain life long contact with Pierre, Jean and Hélène.

On entering the Meurice I was directed to a Flight Lieutenant RAF Intelligence officer, then followed a long interrogation. It appeared that the intelligence officers were looking for Germans trying to infiltrate as former evaders or escapers. I was having some initial difficulty persuading him

---

*P 47 Thunderbolt, single seat escort fighter USAAF

Photograph taken on 2nd September 1944 the day we returned to Paris after liberation. The American is a Thunderbolt pilot on leave.
    From left to right, three of my helpers: Hélène, Pierre and Jacqueline. This was my final day with them before returning to England.

that I belonged to the RAFVR and a member of 106 Squadron. All was finally resolved and I was given a room in this magnificent hotel, my bathroom alone would have made a reasonable lounge. The Germans had left in a hurry and there were uniforms and equipment all over the place. We were ordered not to touch any of the clothing as the items were considered lousy.

Apart from intelligence staff in the hotel there were many evaders, pulled in from the liberated areas of France, and of many nationalities. Given the strange range of clothing, we must have looked a real band of ruffians. We had to stay in the vicinity of the hotel awaiting flight instructions for England.

Homeward bound, 5th September

On the morning of 5th September a number of us were driven to Orly Airport for the flight to RAF Hendon. We boarded a Dakota, the first time I had ever flown without a parachute; we were certainly a motley collection flying for once as passengers. Regardless of the orders at the Meurice, some had acquired German souvenirs such as helmets and forage caps.

We flew back in excellent weather and the sight of the English coast meant a great deal to all. On landing at Hendon, the Dakota taxied to a dispersal point where an RAF lorry was waiting. We alighted to be greeted by an RAF corporal waving a bundle of telegram forms, with the words, 'Remember you are only allowed fifteen words, fifteen words only'. As he kept repeating this we knew without any doubt that we were back in the land of officialdom, in other words, home!

The lorry was scheduled to take us to the Charing Cross Hotel now used as a debriefing centre. It was sheer delight to be back once more on UK roads and there was one amusing incident on our way through London. We were held up at a set of traffic lights and it happened that some of the evaders at the rear of the open lorry were wearing German helmets and a dear old lady waved a walking stick and shouted, 'Your bloody war is over'; we did not have the chance to enlighten her.

On arrival at the Charing Cross Hotel we had a bath. All the clothing we had returned in was taken away for destruction, along with any German souvenirs, the excuse, probably quite correct, was that they would be lousy. This was followed by a long methodical debriefing including all information that might indicate the fate of the rest of the crew. My important question remained unanswered, there was no news of Bill McPhail or the others, they were still posted as missing. After a careful medical check I was told that I would be posted to a hospital for treatment to my shoulder following survivor's leave.

After that first session I was sent across to the Air Ministry at Adastral House for what was termed a technical debriefing with special interest in what I knew about the rocket site at Rouen. I felt that information must have been academic as the Allies had now occupied the area.

At Adastral Rouse I was given travel warrants and departed on survivor's leave. I was also informed that my promotion to Warrant Officer had come through during my absence. Dressed only in battle dress, no cap or insignia, but carrying a note that I was an evader I expected to be taken to task by the military police for being improperly dressed! But I arrived at my parents home in Dundee without incident. The usual instructions were also carried about no talking to the press etc.

The telegram to my parents despatched via RAF Hendon was received by them 24 hours before the official Air Ministry telegram stating my safe return. After a fortnight in Dundee, I was posted to the RAF hospital at Bracla for treatment to my right shoulder. Until the receipt of my telegram my parents only knew that I was missing on operations. Air Ministry could give me no information about the crew other than missing; it was some months later that I discovered Bill McPhail was a POW.

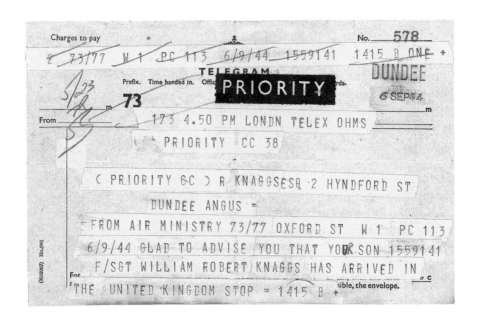

So ended my 'easy trip', the fateful night of 24/25th June 1944 heralded the arrival of major Luftwaffe night-figher forces to defend the Flying bomb (V.I) and rocket (V.II) sites in the Pas-de-Calais and Seine-Maritime Departments. It transpired that Hitler had ordered one third of the night-fighters protecting Germany forward to France to secure his 'secret weapons.' In the following months some 3,000 aircrew would be killed attacking these small and difficult targets .

I lost five close friends that night and over the next eleven weeks had formed and experienced a new and dangerous friendship with the men and women of Occupied France who were to risk their lives assisting an unknown airman. Such activities inevitably resulted in the formation of the Royal Air Force's Escaping Society in September 1945 thus ensuring that such friendships would indeed last a lifetime.

It should be remembered that for every known 'Helper' this probably meant whole families or family groups were involved, such knowledge placing at risk at least 50,000 throughout the various countries.

One sad task remained to be completed during my survivor's leave; that of contacting the families of the rest of the crew still posted as missing and including at that time Bill McPhail the Flight Engineer. I called upon Bill's parents in Paisley to advise them that I was certain he had baled out although I had been unable to find him. On visiting Hugh Smith's mother in Glasgow and before I could get beyond the introduction she told me that she knew Hugh was dead and that he had died at midnight on the 24th June. It was uncanny, she had no way of knowing the exact time we were attacked over the target or even that we were operating that night. She said that she had been awakened at midnight by a cow lowing and knew Hugh had gone. She lived in the centre of Glasgow far from any cattle and of course this was 24 hours before she received the Air Ministry telegram reporting Hugh missing from operations. In Scottish folklore the sound of cattle lowing at night is reputed to be a sign of death.

I wrote to the other relatives in England and Australia trying to balance the possibility of some hope without giving any real encouragement being convinced that Bill McPhail and myself were the only survivors. When writing these letters one always had an unanswerable question in mind, 'why me', why should I be the one destined to live out of that close band of friends? Kind replies were received from all the families and Bill Beutel's parents invited me to take up residence in Australia after the war. I was sorely tempted but eventually declined the offer.

Gerrard 9234

Tel. No. HOLBORN 3434

Ext. ....

AIR MINISTRY,

ADASTRAL HOUSE,

KINGSWAY, W.C.2.

P.419246/4/P.4.Cas.

(Casualty Branch)
73-77 Oxford Street,
London, W.1.

18th January, 1945

Dear Flight Sergeant Knaggs,

I am unable to trace any statement of yours in this Department and am consequently writing to ask if you can give us any particulars of the loss of your aircraft on 24th/25th June last.

We should like to know where the aircraft crashed, for instance, and if you are aware of the fate of the other members of the crew besides Sergeant McPhail who is a prisoner of war.

French reports of what may have been your aircraft mention the burial of four bodies in the vicinity of Bully. No identification was possible owing to the removal of all means of identification by the Boche but they do say that one of them was well over six feet in height.

Did you have anyone in your crew who would answer to this description?

Congratulations on your own escape.

Yours sincerely,

L. G. BRISTOWE.

1559141 Flight Sergeant W.R. Knaggs,
2 Hyndford Street,
Dundee.

Back in the United Kingdom I was an aircrew member without a crew, part of my life had gone. With the loss of my friends, so whither now; 'evaders' were not allowed to return to operations over Europe. I was posted to 72 Base Headquarters as Unit Warrant Officer. As the Allies advanced I was involved in photographic flights over reoccupied territory. I remained earmarked for 'J' Force, but with Japan capitulating I left the Royal Air Force in July 1946 and returned to my old company in the wine trade.

THEY LIE AT REST
St SEVER CEMETERY ROUEN

The graves of:
P/O Stan Wright, F/Sgt. Les McGregor, F/Sgt. Bill Beutel

Not shown in this photograph but buried in the same row lie:
F/Sgt. Hughie Smith and F/Sgt. Nick Clarke.

Photograph 1981

*The lake at Enghiem-les-Bains where we cycled every Sunday morning.
The casino in the background was the local Gestapo HQ. My 'helper' Jean
Collin in the foreground.*

*Photograph taken July 1975, the distant background very different to
1944.*

The helpers in happier times

Jean Collin and Hélène Galy married after the war although by then my company had transferred me to Malta and thence to East Africa. Contact was maintained by letter and the details only limited by my indifferent French when writing to both them and Pierre. I enjoyed regular correspondence with Jacqueline Tibbatts until 1955.

The Galy and Collin families prospered, Jacqueline worked with the United Nations, initially in Geneva and then in West Africa. Her last letter was received in 1955 when all contact was lost with both myself and her old friends in France; it has remained a mystery.

On my return to the United Kingdom in 1961 and through my membership of the RAF Escaping Society it was a great pleasure to meet once again the Galy and Collin families on both visits to France and England. After my retirement it was a privilege to entertain them and welcome them to Scotland.

When Pierre Galy's son Philippe married his wife Agnes, a delightful lady who taught English, it at last gave me an opportunity with Agnes as my interpreter to convey my real appreciation for what they had all done and risked.

While I was in East Africa in the fifties Jacqueline Tibbatts parents arrived in London; I had no knowledge of their movements or word from Jacqueline. The parents apparently were in straitened circumstances. The Society found a flat for them in London and furniture was gifted by a well known company through the good offices of Rotary. Mrs Tibbatts fell ill and died in 1958, her husband followed shortly after; the Society took care of all the funeral arrangements.

*Pierre,
Jacqueline and
Hélène at the
Galy home in
Ermont.
October 1944.*

*Pierre Galy and
Jacqueline
Tibbats outside
my 'safe house'
in Ermont.
December 1944.*

Jean and Hélène Collin at the British Embassy in Paris September 1976, a reception to honour those who had assisted Allied airmen to evade capture. Organised by the RAF Escaping Society and hosted by the British Ambassador.

The 'safe house' in Ermont, the top flat where Bill Knaggs stayed during July and August 1944. Jean and Hélène Collin can be seen in the bottom left hand corner. Photograph taken in September 1976.

Charges to pay

POST OFFICE   A ONE +   MD

6 77 W 1 PC 988 ONE 10/2/45 1125822 9/2/45 1421

TELEGRAM

Prefix. Time handed in. Office of Origin and Service Instructions. Words

46

From   446 5/10 PM LONDON-TELEX OHMS 59   To

PRIORITY-CC W S McPHAIL ESQ 6 CALEDONIA ST

PAISLEY RENFREWSHIRE. =

FROM AIR MINISTRY 77 OXFORD ST   W.1 PC 988

10/2/45 THE NAME OF YOUR SON 1125822 SGT WILLIA

STEVENSON McPHAIL WAS INCLUDED IN A POLISH F

PROVISIONAL GOVERNMENT BROADCAST ON 9/2/45 AS BEI

SAFE IN LUBIN STOP TEXT OF BROADCAST WILL BE or c

POSTED STOP NO OFFICIAL INFORMATION YET RECEIVED

STOP = 1421 A +   LIMITED

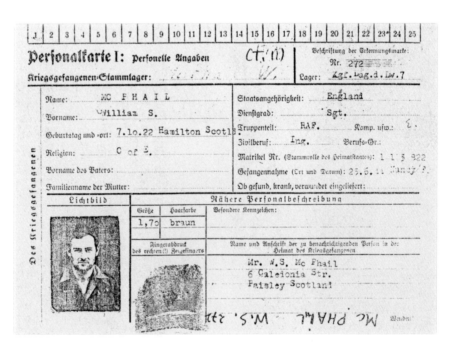

Flight Sergeant Bill McPhail

Bill McPhail was an excellent Flight Engineer, a former apprentice marine engineer before volunteering for aircrew, he was completely at home with engines; we were in good hands.

Bill unfortunately died suddenly in April 1984 and his account of the events on and after Pommeréval will never be known. I just have a few sketchy details. Unusually we two survivors finished up as one evader and one escaper. Following the instruction to bale out, Bill reached the forward compartment and was right behind me when I jumped. Our Lancaster exploded immediately after Bill baled out and he had the misfortune to land in the trees surrounding the target. He was picked up after dawn and taken to the nearest German headquarters in a lorry along with four bodies, almost certainly from our crew. The Gestapo gave him a rough time in their quest for information before he was transferred to *Stalag Luft 7* in Silesia. We will never know the real horrors of his escape through Poland and Russia to Odesssa or the courage and endurance that saw him through that journey.

Left to right: Bill McPhail with wife Mary and Bill Knaggs.
106 Squadron Reunion Woodhall Spa 1983.
This was the last occasion I was to see Bill. He died suddenly in 1984.

In February 1945 as the Germans marched their POWs west in the face of the Russian advance Bill escaped and headed east through Poland and Russia eventually returning home via Odessa. He experienced dreadful conditions during those winter months and said but for the Poles and the Polish Underground fighters he would have died, the Russian troops were not interested in giving aid. Information about Bill's escape was picked up from a radio broadcast by the Provisional Polish Government of the 9th February 1945; this message was passed on to his mother by the Air Ministry. During his journey through Poland he was able to assist a Miss Walker, a former British agent caught up in the outbreak of war. She was then 67 and had helped a number of Allied Servicemen down the Polish underground escape route. Along with three other airmen she came out with Bill dressed as a POW.

On meeting Bill in 1945 I found that our wireless operator Les McGregor had been killed in the attack. Bill's death was a great blow as on retirement we had hoped to arrange regular meetings. We were both members of 106 Squadron Association. He was the last link; at least for all too short a period we knew that special friendship that bound bomber crews together.

106 lives on in the form of the 106 Squadron Association thanks to founder member Des Richards in his combination of secretary / treasurer and historian. Aircrew were 'birds of passage', few survived to complete a tour of operations and therefore saw only a fragment of squadron life. We are deeply indebted to Des Richards who spent three years with the squadron as a member of ground staff and has since spent a lifetime compiling a history, much of it photographic and entailing numerous visits to the former Occupied countries. He has built up a lasting friendship with the people who have been responsible for looking after with such great care the graves of 106 aircrews. It was the men and women on the ground staff, the backbone of any squadron who kept the 'birds flying' and who are all too often forgotten.

The Résistance Movement –
Tedder and Eisenhower Certificates:

After the War the British and American governments authorised the issue of documents known respectively as Tedder and Eisenhower Certificates being an expression of gratitude to those in the Occupied countries who at great risk had helped Allied servicemen to evade capture. The secretary of the RAF Escaping Society, Mrs Elizabeth Lucas Harrison, MBE, persuaded Msr Michel Tabarant to let me have copies of these very personal papers. Michel did in fact send copies of the Certificates issued to both himself, his father Jean and his uncle Maurice Dupuis. Michel's aunt Genevière Dupuis-Tabarant also received the Eisenhower Certificate, a very gallant family indeed.

Although I did not pass through the hands of the Tabarants I have included their details to emphasise the work such families throughout occupied Europe were engaged in.

The family assisted at least 9 aircrew, 2 Canadians, 2 Americans and 5 British, before starting on their escape routes home these airmen were hidden on the Tabarant farm at Crouy near Soissons. Disaster struck on 31st July 1944 when the farm was raided by the Gestapo. The entire family were arrested and taken to Gestapo Headquarters at Soissons, the next day Michel, Maurice Dupuis and aunt Genevière were transferred to prison. Maurice Dupuis was sent on to the concentration camp at Dachau and died there in 1945 without having revealed any of his Résistance activities. Maurice was chief of the Northern Sector of the Résistance at Soissons; Maurice was awarded posthumously France highest decoration, The Legion d'Honneur and received both the Tedder and Eisenhower Certificates. Michel and Genevière left prison on the eve of the American Army entry into Soissons.

At the time the farm was raided the family still had one evader, F/Lt. John Collar; he was the only person to escape, finding his way to Paris where he stayed until the city was liberated. One of Michel's 'guests' was F/O. Bill Alliston, later to be one of my friends in the Escaping Society and who served at one stage as the Society Chairman.

The following is an extract from a letter received from Michel Tabarant with the copies of the Tedder Certificates.

The first airman helped by my family was a Canadian Sqn. Ldr. Fletcher Taylor, pilot of a Wellington bomber shot down during the night of 15.4.43 near St. Ouentin. He arrived very early in the

Another evader in the safe hands of Michel Tabarrat at the farm of Mont de Vauxrot at Crouy, 8 k NE of Soissons.
   From left to right: R.G Symons, USAF radio-operator on a B 24 (Liberator), Michel Tabarant.
                    December 1943. (Photo Michel Tabarant)

morning in my uncle Maurice Dupuis farmyard at Crouy, near Soissons. At that time we did not know of an escape line and he was sent to Switzerland via my parents home at Laon, then through Reims, Dijon, Dole and Pontarlier. *In January 1944 he re-entered France to gain Spain and returned to the UK in February 1944.

The 2nd airman was an American, G. Symons, a radio operator on a USAF B.24 (Liberator bomber) he arrived end December 1943. We then had an escape line via Paris, eventually arriving in the UK.

In April 1944, 3 British officers, F/Lt. John Collar, F/O. Bill Alliston and F/O. Maurice Steel, Halifax bomber crew survivors, all stayed with us on the farm for several weeks, often joined by two other airmen hidden in a nearby-village, Charles Clount, an American pilot of a P 47 (USAF Thunderbolt fighter bomber) and Arnold Green another American who had joined the RCAF. On the 31st July 1944 when we were arrested by the Gestapo only Collar was still with us at the farm. He was the only one able to escape. The whole family was taken to Gestapo HQ at Soissons. My uncle and myself were transferred to prison next evening. My uncle was deported and died in Dachau concentration camp on 19.5.45. My aunt and myself left prison on 26.8.44 when the US Army was on the point of entering Soissons. We were very lucky.

The extract from Michel's letter gives but a brief outline of his own and family's activities, but given those dangerous years and the Germans ruthless determination to stamp out all forms of resistance, one can only guess at some of the tensions and risks taken to hide and transfer airmen across France with, in many cases, tragic consequences for the helpers.

I dropped into France shortly after the Résistance groups had been instructed from London to close down the escape routes into Spain and that Allied airmen were to be held in safe areas pending the arrival of the liberating armies. The Tabarant family had no connection with my term as an evader but I felt it necessary to give, be it but a sketch of their actions, as a reminder of the enterprise shown by those who risked death in the cause of freedom.

---

*The normal escape route was through France and over the Pyrénées into Spain and home via Gibraltar. The Spanish were in no way helpful on the way to Gibraltar.

This No. 10 Squadron Halifax shot down by night-fighter on 10.5.44 crashed near village of Leschelles, 5 k SW from Soissons. Crew of 8, 3 were killed, 2 became POWs and 3 were evaders, 2 of whom are shown above.

Left to right: Msr Henri de Brossard (acting as lorry driver) F/O. Maurice Stell (Nav.) F/O. Bill Alliston (mid-upper gunner). (Photo M. Tabarant 12.5.44.)

The evaders from No. 10 Squadron Halifax at the farm of Mont de Vauxrot, Crouy, 8 k NE of Soissons. Left to right: Maurice Steel, Michel Tabarant, F/O. Bill Alliston, F/Lt. John Collar. (Photo Michel Tabarant May 1944.)

This certificate is awarded to

Monsieur Maurice Dupuis

as a token of gratitude for and appreciation

of the help given to the Sailors, Soldiers

and Airmen of the British Commonwealth

of Nations, which enabled them to escape

from, or evade capture by the enemy.

1939-1945

Air Chief Marshal,
Deputy Supreme Commander,
Allied Expeditionary Force

Maurice Dupuis, uncle to Michel Tabarant was Chief of the Northern Sector of the Résistance at Soissons (Aisne). He was arrested on 31st July 1944, deported to Dachu concentration camp on the 16th August 1944 and died on the 18th May 1945. He received both Tedder and Eisenhower Certificates, was posthumously nominated as Chevalier of the Legion d'Honneur and awarded the Medal of Freedom from the United States Government.

EXTRAIT

du DÉCRET en date du 6 Août 1955

publié au J. O. du 17 Août 1955

portant   nominations dans la LEGION D'HONNEUR

__ARTICLE I__ er Sont nommés dans l'Ordre National de la Légion
d'Honneur :

AU GRADE DE CHEVALIER

A TITRE POSTHUME

. . . .

DUPUIS Maurice - Sous-Lieutenant -

"Magnifique patriote, membre des Forces Françaises Combattantes.
"Arrêté pour faits de Résistance le 31 Juillet 1944, a été interné
"jusqu'au 15 Août 1944, puis déporté le 16 Août 1944 dans un camp de
"concentration, où il est mort glorieusement pour la France, le 18
"Mai 1945."

. . . .

CES NOMINATIONS COMPORTENT :

1°/- L'attribution de la croix de guerre avec palme, à titre posthume,
elles annulent les citations accordées pour les mêmes faits.

2°/- L'attribution de la Médaille de la Résistance, à titre posthume,
(application des prescriptions de l'article 9 de la Loi N° 48-
1251 du 6 Août 1948).

Par le Président de la République   signé : René COTY
Le Président du Conseil des Ministres
        signé : Edgar FAURE
                                          Le Ministre de la Défense
        POUR AMPLIATION   Nationale et des Forces Armées
L'Administrateur civil de 1ère classe   signé : P. KOENIG
            CHERRIERE
    Chef du Bureau des Décorations
    P.O.Le Capitaine LAMOTHE,

This certificate is awarded to

Monsieur Jean Tabarant

as a token of gratitude for and appreciation

of the help given to the Sailors, Soldiers

and Airmen of the British Commonwealth

of Nations, which enabled them to escape

from, or evade capture by the enemy.

Air Chief Marshal,
Deputy Supreme Commander,
1939-1945　　　　　Allied Expeditionary Force

I did not have the privilege of meeting this brave family but through the medium of Mrs Elizabeth Harrison MBE, Secretary of the RAF Escaping Society, Msr Michel Tabarant kindly sent copies of these personal Tedder Certificates in respect of himself and his father Msr Jean Tabarant with the proviso that they could only be used in this publication. Michel's father, uncle Maurice Dupuis and aunt Genevieve Dupuis-Tabarant were also recipients of both Tedder and Eisenhower Certificates.

This certificate is awarded to

Monsieur Michel Tabarant

as a token of gratitude for and appreciation of the help given to the Sailors, Soldiers and Airmen of the British Commonwealth of Nations, which enabled them to escape from, or evade capture by the enemy.

Air Chief Marshal,
Deputy Supreme Commander,
Allied Expeditionary Force

1939-1945

Royal Air Force's Escaping Society

The Society was formed in 1945 by Lord Portal, then Chief of Air Staff, all members are airmen of the Royal and Dominion Air Forces who were forced down over enemy occupied areas and successfully escaped from captivity or evaded capture to reach the safety of Allied territory. Evasion in almost every instance due to the courage of the men and women of the Occupied countries under the penalty of certain death.

The objects of the Society were simple, to give assistance to the widows and orphans of those who lost their lives helping Allied airmen to evade capture, and to foster the firm friendships formed between the helpers and evaders.

Immediately after the war the Society had contact with over 14,000 helpers. A representative in each of the former Occupied countries advises of cases in need, the very nature of the people who assisted our airmen means they are unlikely to request help themselves; at its peak grantees totalled 285. Christmas cards were despatched each year to known helpers and these did elicit some emotional replies and surprise that the Society continued to remember and care over so many years.

2,803 airmen from the Royal and Dominion Air Forces, 2,000 from the United States Air Force and 150 escapees from POW camps were returned safely to the United Kingdom; the prospect for our helpers was either execution or concentration camp.

The Society arranged numerous visits to the former Occupied countries and entertained helpers in the United Kingdom over the years, all memorable occasions. Through our Speakers' Panel we continue to remind the public of the extraordinary courage of the helpers.

Exactly 50 years plus one day from its formation the Society held a final AGM on 16th September 1995 during a three day series of functions in Lincoln. At the final dinner held at the Royal Air Force College, Cranwell, it seemed fitting that our distinguished guest was the then current Chief of Air Staff, Sir Michael Graydon.

The AGM was not the final moment as it was agreed to continue with our other title, the RAF Escaping Society Charitable Fund until such time as the Trustees deemed it necessary to cease.

In 1945 following discussions between the Air Ministry and the Government, a Certificate was sent to over 30,000 helpers to thank them for their assistance to Allied airmen, these were known as the Tedder and Eisenhower Certificates respectively.

ROYAL AIR FORCES ESCAPING SOCIETY
(1945-1995)
206 BROMPTON ROAD LONDON SW3 2BQ
TELEPHONE NUMBER   0171-584 5378

LAYING   UP   OF   THE   STANDARD

LINCOLN CATHEDRAL   17th SEPTEMBER 1995

THE LAST ACT

Members of the RAF Escaping Society and their helpers visiting the Mont Valerien Memorial in Paris on 15th September 1990.

The party are listening to an interpretation of the Plaque inscription.

The plaque covers the spot where 4,500 French men and women were shot for Résistance activities during the Occupation. Even today there is a strange sombre silence, not even a birdsong can be heard.

Extract from – Night Raid Report No. 642

Bomber command report on night operations, 24/25th June 1944.

POMMERÉVAL (extract for Pommeréval attack only)

SUMMARY

1. 7 launching-sites in the Pas de Calais were strongly attacked in cloudless weather. 5 were damaged. Opposition was severe, and 23 of the 739 aircraft engaged were lost. Mosquitos attacked Berlin, and our minelayers and fighters were active. One more aircraft was lost on subsidiary operations.

WEATHER FORECAST

2. Bases: Mainly fit, with well broken st-cu. Local smoke in Midlands. Continent: Little or no cloud in N. France and Belgium. Medium cloud and st-cu. will increase eastwards, affecting the Ruhr soon after midnight.

PLAN OF ATTACK

3. Pommeréval 5 Group technique. 5 OBOE Mosquitos were to mark each A/P with yellow TI. The details of the method to be employed were to be decided by the A.O.C. 5 Group. A Controller was to direct each attack H = 2355 at Pommeréval.

SORTIES

4. Pommeréval	Aircraft Despatched	Attacked Primary	Attacked Alternative	Aborted	Missing
	111	109	0	2	4

WEATHER EXPERIENCED

5. Bases: Broken st. cu. and medium cloud. Moderate to good visibility. Targets: All cloudless. Slight haze. New Moon, setting at 0045. Wind at 15,000': 300 /30 m.p.h.

NARRATIVE OF ATTACKS

6. All the attacks were reported to be accurate and concentrated.

DAY RECONNAISSANCE

7. Pommeréval Many craters occurred in the target area. 4 target buildings, 10 houses and several other installations within the perimeter wire were destroyed or damaged.

ENEMY DEFENCES

8.   Fighters, searchlights and light guns co-operated effectively against our aircraft, especially while the moon was up (i.e., against the forces visiting Prouville, Pommeréval and Rimeux). There was no cloud to hamper them. The fighters were airborne early, coming from their bases between Le Culot and Chateaudun to beacons in the Lille-Cambrai-St.Quentin area. They arrived in time to chase the Pommeréval force homewards to St. Valery, and met Prouville and Rimeux forces over their targets.

ENEMY AIRCRAFT DESTROYED

9.   A Lancaster returning from Pommeréval destroyed a Ju 88 and a Me 109, and other Lancaster shot down a second Me 109.

CASUALTIES

10.   22 of the 739 aircraft detailed for the Pas de Calais targets were lost. This was the first night on which severe opposition had been encountered in this area. At Pommeréval 2 bombers were lost to fighter and 2 to flak. No returning aircraft was seriously damaged.

Extract from Night Raid Report No. 642.

Bomber command report on night operations, 24/25th June, 1944.

PROUVILLE : MIDDEL STRAETE : LE GRAND ROSSIGNOL : RIMEUX : FLEURS : POMMERÉVAL : BAMIERES.

SUMMARY

1.   7 launching-sites in the Pas de Calais were strongly attacked in cloudless weather. 5 were damaged. Opposition was severe, and 23 of the 739 aircraft engaged were lost. Mosquitos attacked Berlin, and our minelayers and fighters were active. One more aircraft was lost on subsidiary operations.

WEATHER FORECAST

2.   Bases: Mainly fit, with well broken st-cu. Local smoke in Midlands. Continent: Little or no cloud in N. France and Belgium. Medium cloud and st-cu. Will increase eastwards, affecting the Ruhr soon after midnight.

PLANS OF ATTACK

3.   **Prouville:& Pommeréval** 5 Group technique. 5 OBOE Mosquitos were to mark each A/P with yellow T/I. The other details of the method to be employed were to be decided by the A.O.C. 5 Group. A Controller was to direct each attack. H .- 0015 at Prouville; 2355 at Pommeréval.

4.   **Middel Straete** OBOE ground-marking. 5 OBOE Mosquitos were to drop red TI at the centre of which the main force were to aim. H = 0125

5.   **Le Grand Rossiqnol: Rimeux & Bamieres**. As for Middel Straete, except that backers-up were to aim greens at the centre of the reds, and the main forces were to bomb on the centre of reds or greens, or blindly. H = 0300 at Le Grand Rossignol; 0030 at Rimeux; 0145 at Bamieres.

6.   **Fleurs**: Controlled OBOE ground-marking. As for Middel Straete; except that a Master Bomber or his deputy was to keep the A/P marked with greens, and the main force were to aim at the centre of his markers. If the OBOE marking was accurate, the Master Bomber would remain silent; but if necessary, yellows were to be used to distinguish the A/P. H= 0315.

SORTIES		Despatched	Attacked Primary	Attacked Alt.	Abort.	Missing.
7.	Prouville	112	106	2	4	13
	Middel Straete	85	84	0	1	0
	Le Grand Rossignol	107	107	0	0	0
	Rimeux	107	107	0	0	4
	Fleurs	107	102	0	5	1
	Pomméréval	111	109	0	2	4
	Bamieres	110	108	0	2	0
	TOTAL	739	723	2	14	22

WEATHER EXPERIENCED
8.　Bases: Broken st. cu. and medium cloud. Moderate to good visibility. Targets: All cloudless. Slight haze. New moon, setting at 0045. Wind at 15,000'; 300 /30 m.p.h., except at Flers (270 /20 m.p.h).

NARRATIVE OF ATTACKS
9.　All the attacks were reported to be accurate and concentrated.

DAY RECONNOISSANCE
10.　**Prouville** All visible craters were to the R. of the target.

11.　**Middel Straete** Several new craters occurred in the target area including 3 hits on the launching point.

12.　**Le Grand Rossiqnol** Many bombs had fallen on the target, including 5 on the square building, 1 on the launching platform and 20 on the road which traverses the target.

13.　**Rimeux** This target also suffered severely. 2 hits wrecked the base of the launching point, which also sustained 3 near misses. The square building suffered roof damage.

14.　**Fleurs** This attack fell to the S. & E. of the target, which appeared not to have been damaged.

15.　**Pommeréval** Many craters occurred in the target area. 4 target buildings, 10 houses and several other installations within the perimeter wire were destroyed or damaged.

16.　**Bamieres** 60 fresh craters were visible in the area of this target. The square building was completely destroyed, and the launching point sustained a very near miss.

ENEMY DEFENCES

17.   Fighters, searchlights and light guns co-operated effectively against our aircraft, especially while the moon was up (i.e., against the forces visiting Prouville, Pommeréval and Rimeux). There was no cloud to hamper them. The fighters were airborne early, coming from their bases between Le Culot and Chateaudun to beacons in the Lille-Cambrai-St.Quentin area. They arrived in time to chase the Pommeréval force homewards to St. Valery, and met the Prouville and Rimeux forces over their targets. The Prouville attack unfortunately lasted for over half an hour, and the fighters destroyed: 5 aircraft over the target during the last 20 minutes. The ground defences left most of the shooting to the fighters who were assisted by the accurate work of the searchlight crews.

ENEMY AIRCRAFT DESTROYED

18.   A Lancaster returning from Pommeréval destroyed a Ju 88 and a Me 109, and another Lancaster shot down a second Me 109. A SERRATE Mosquito of 100 Group shot down a Ju 88

CASUALTIES

19.   22 of the 739 aircraft detailed for the Pas de Calais targets were lost (3.0%). This was the first night on which severe opposition had been encountered in this area. 13 of the losses were sustained by the Prouville force as has been explained, the attack was unduly prolonged, and fighters claimed at least 8 victims and the light guns 2 more. At Pommeréval 2 bombers were lost to fighters and 2 to flak. At Rimeux 1 fell to a fighter and another to flak. The causes of the remaining 6 losses are not known. No returning aircraft was seriously damaged.

Extract from operations record book –

49 squadron, RAF Fiskerton

24/25th June 1944 –
    Rocket Construction Site Pommeréval, Seine-Maritime Department.

Lancaster	Pilot	
LL 976 Lacy*	21.58–01.49.	Pommeréval 00.04, 6,750 ft. 1st wave. Vis. good, no cloud. Bombed green TIs. River seen of approach to target area. Bombing well concentrated around green TIs. Route good and avoided all defend areas. Fighters had every advantage.
ND5 12 Pederson	21.57–01.45.	Pommeréval 00.08, 6,500 ft. 3rd wave. Clear but some haze, vis. good. Target well marked. We bombed green TI. 3 large explosions seen. Ground seen at times. Road seen quite clearly. 3 sightings of enemy aircraft.
ND 383 Dickson	22.00–01.52.	Pommeréval 00.08, 8,200 ft. 2nd wave. Clear, vis. good. Bombed green TIs as directed. Bombing well concentrated but marking of target very late. consider attack took place too early as it was quite light.
ND 787 Edwards	21.56–02.02	Pommeréval 00.07 and half, 6,000 ft. 1st wave. Clear but smoke. Vis. good. Bombimg concentrated on TIs. Fighter activity over target considerable. Some heavy flak but ineffective at our height.
JB 701 Powell*	22.01–01.47	Pommeréval 00.08, 6,200 ft. 1st wave. Clear but smoke. Bombed green TIs. Gee confirmed. Weather conditions favourable to enemy-half light. If orbiting had not been ordered, force would have left target before fighters arrived.
ND 471 Arnold	22.08–01.46	Pommeréval 00.11, 8,000 ft. 3rd wave. Clear some haze, vis. good. Bombed centre of 2 green TIs. and red spot fires. Target very well marked. At least 6 sticks of bomb landed around the markers. 3 orange/red explosions seen from coast on return at about 0025. Heavy flak over target.

JB 473 Jordon   22.03–01.57 Pommeréval 00.08, 7,500 ft. 3rd wave
Hazy. Bombed green TIs. Could not see
ground detail owing to photo flashes bursting.
Bombs seemed well concentrated on target
indicators.

IM 572 Taylor   22.11–   Crew on 1st operation – failed to return.

ND 957 Poole   22.06–01.58 Pommeréval 00.05, 9,000 ft. 2nd wave. (crew
on 1st operation)
Bombed 1 green TI. Clear, good vis. Marking
very late, but bombing appeared concentrated
on it. Routing good.

ND 647 Rowley   22.04–01.40 Pommeréval 00.08, 7,300 ft. 3rd wave.
Vis good. Bombed concentration green TIs.
Trip good on the whole but marking late.
Attack concentrated on markers.

VB 178 Buchanan* 22.09–01.42 Pommeréval 00.06, 7,750 ft. 2nd wave.
Clear but smokey. Bombed 3 red spot fires
and 1 green TI Bombing appeared to be
concentrated around markers which were
rather obscured by smoke from explosions.
An uneventful trip.

IM 541 McCracken 22.07–02.01 Pommeréval 00.08, 8,500 ft. 2nd wave. (crew
on 1st operation)
Bombed centre of cluster green TIs. Weather
over target fairly good. Had to orbit and come
back on original heading. Ordered to bomb
green TIs. No flak no explosions seen.

ND 684 Appleyard* 2210–0131 Pommeréval 00.02, 7,000 ft. 1st wave.
Clear but slight haze. Vis. good. Bombed red
& green TIs and one building seen visually.
Own bombs believed to have started fire. Red
& green lit up this building and bomb aimer
says that bombs hit it.

---

* These crews failed to return from subsequent operations.